Sarah Hill

Pure & Simple
Healthy Kids Cuisine
Organic Recipes for Baby and Toddler

Table of Content

Introduction

Welcome to "Pure & Simple: Healthy Kids Cuisine"—your essential guide to nurturing your little ones with meals that are as nutritious as they are delightful. As a parent, you are aware that providing your kids with a healthy diet is one of the most significant things you can do for their well-being. This book is designed to take the stress out of mealtime and transform it into an enjoyable experience for both you and your child.

We recognize that introducing new foods and textures to your child can be difficult at times, but it is also a wonderful chance to broaden their taste and promote wholesome eating habits from an early age. In "Pure & Simple," we've crafted a diverse range of recipes that cater to the unique nutritional needs of babies and toddlers, ensuring they receive balanced meals that are full of flavor and goodness.

This cookbook features meticulously planned for breakfast, lunch, and dinner, tailored specifically for different stages of your child's development. Whether you're making a creamy Avocado and Banana Mash for your baby or a delicious Zucchini Waffle for your toddler, each recipe is designed to be simple, wholesome, and irresistibly tasty.

Understanding that every child is unique, we've included sections dedicated to dietary restrictions and preferences. There are lots of delectable recipes available to meet your child's dietary requirements, whether they are vegetarian, vegan, dairy-free, or gluten-free. From Vegan Lentil Lasagna to Gluten-Free Quinoa and Veggie Bites, every meal is crafted to be safe and suitable for your child's diet.

We also believe that snacks and desserts are an important part of a balanced diet. Our creative snack ideas, like Veggie Pinwheels and Cheese and Pineapple Cubes, are perfect for little hands and growing appetites. And for those special moments, our healthy desserts, such as Vegan Avocado Chocolate Pudding and Gluten-Free Apple and Carrot Muffins, are sure to bring smiles to your children's faces.

"Pure & Simple: Healthy Kids Cuisine" is more than just a cookbook, it is a traveling companion that will help you transform mealtimes into a treasured part of your everyday schedule. We hope these recipes inspire you to cook with love and creativity, turning every meal into a culinary adventure for your family.

So grab your apron, gather your little sous-chefs, and let's embark on this delightful journey of wholesome and delicious cooking together. Here's to happy, healthy eating and many wonderful moments around the family table!

BABY

BREAKFAST

Avocado and Banana Mash

Ingredients:

·1 ripe avocado
·1 ripe banana

Practical Tips for Preparing and Planning Meals:

Batch Preparation: Prepare multiple servings at once and store in the refrigerator for quick access.
Pre-Mashing: Pre-mash the fruits and store them in small portions to make serving easier.
Texture Variation: For older babies, you can leave some small chunks for added texture and to help them develop chewing skills.

Storage Information:

Refrigerator: Store the prepared mash in an airtight container for up to 1 day. Note that avocado can brown quickly, so adding a little lemon juice can help preserve the color (use sparingly and only if your baby tolerates citrus).
Freezer: While avocado and banana mash is best fresh, you can freeze it for up to 1 month. Freeze in small portions and thaw in the refrigerator before serving.

Instructions:

1. **Prepare the Ingredients:**
Cut the avocado in half, remove the pit, and scoop the flesh into a small bowl.
Peel the banana and slice it into the bowl with the avocado.
2. **Mash and Combine:**
Use a fork or a potato masher to thoroughly mash the avocado and banana together until smooth and well combined.
3. **Serve:**
Serve the mash immediately or store as needed.

Nutritional Value per Serving (Approximate):
Calories: 160 Proteins: 2g Fats: 8g Carbohydrates: 22g

5 Minutes

20 Minutes

2 servings

Apple and Cinnamon Quinoa

Ingredients:

· *1/4 cup quinoa*
· *1/2 cup water*
· *1 small apple, peeled, cored, and finely chopped*
· *1/4 teaspoon ground cinnamon*

Practical Tips for Preparing and Planning Meals:

Batch Cooking: *Prepare a larger quantity and store in the refrigerator for up to 3 days. Reheat individual servings as needed.*
Quick Apple Prep: *Use a food processor to finely chop the apple for faster preparation.*
Consistency Adjustment: *Add a little more water or breast milk/formula to adjust the consistency if needed.*

Storage Information:

Refrigerator: *Store the prepared quinoa mixture in an airtight container for up to 3 days.*
Freezer: *Portion the quinoa mixture into small, airtight containers or ice cube trays and freeze for up to 1 month. Thaw in the refrigerator overnight before reheating.*

Instructions:

1. **Prepare the Quinoa:**
Rinse the quinoa thoroughly under cold water to remove any bitterness.
2. **Cook the Quinoa:**
In a small saucepan, combine the rinsed quinoa and water.
Bring to a boil, then reduce the heat to low, cover, and simmer for about 10 minutes.
3. **Add Apple and Cinnamon:**
Add the finely chopped apple and ground cinnamon to the saucepan.
Stir well, cover, and continue to simmer for another 10 minutes, or until the quinoa is tender and the apple pieces are soft.
4. **Mash and Cool:**
Once cooked, mash the mixture lightly with a fork or potato masher to reach the desired consistency for your baby.
Allow the mixture to cool to a safe temperature before serving.

Nutritional Value per Serving (Approximate):
Calories: 180 Proteins: 4g Fats: 3g Carbohydrates: 35g

5 Minutes

0 Minutes

2 servings

Blueberry Yogurt

Ingredients:

·1/2 cup plain whole milk yogurt
·1/4 cup fresh or frozen blueberries
(thawed if frozen)

Practical Tips for Preparing and Planning Meals:

Batch Preparation: Prepare multiple servings and store them in the refrigerator for quick access.
Texture Variation: For older babies, you can leave some blueberry chunks for added texture.
Flavor Variety: Experiment with other fruits like strawberries, peaches, or mangoes for different flavors.

Storage Information:

Refrigerator: Store the prepared blueberry yogurt in an airtight container for up to 2 days.
Freezer: While yogurt can change texture when frozen, you can freeze the mixture in small portions for up to 1 month. Thaw in the refrigerator before serving.

Instructions:

1. **Prepare the Blueberries:**
In case of using fresh blueberries, wash them thoroughly.
If using frozen blueberries, thaw them completely.
2. **Blend the Ingredients:**
In a small bowl, combine the yogurt and blueberries.
Mash the blueberries with a fork or blend them with the yogurt until smooth.
3. **Serve:**
Serve immediately or store as needed.

Nutritional Value per Serving (Approximate):
Calories: 100 Proteins: 4g Fats: 3g Carbohydrates: 15g

5 Minutes

0 Minutes

2 servings

Strawberry Banana Smoothie

Ingredients:

·1 ripe banana
·1/2 cup fresh or frozen strawberries
(thawed if frozen)
·1/2 cup whole milk or plain yogurt
·1/4 cup water or breast milk/formula
(optional, for consistency)

Practical Tips for Preparing and Planning Meals:

Batch Preparation: Prepare a larger batch and store in the refrigerator for a quick grab-and-go meal.
Smoothie Popsicles: Pour the smoothie into popsicle molds and freeze for a refreshing treat.
Consistency Adjustment: Adjust the thickness of the smoothie by adding more liquid as needed.

Storage Information:

Refrigerator: Store the prepared smoothie in an airtight container for up to 2 days.
Freezer: Pour into ice cube trays or popsicle molds and freeze for up to 1 month. Thaw individual portions in the refrigerator or enjoy as frozen treats.

Instructions:

1. **Prepare the Ingredients:**
After peeling, chop the banana into large pieces.
Wash the strawberries thoroughly and remove the stems.
2. **Blend the Smoothie:**
In a blender, combine the banana, strawberries, and whole milk or yogurt. Blend until smooth. If the mixture is too thick, add water or breast milk/formula a little at a time until the desired consistency is reached.
3. **Serve:**
Pour the smoothie into a cup and serve immediately

Nutritional Value per Serving (Approximate):
Calories: 80 Proteins: 2g Fats: 0.5g Carbohydrates: 18g

Pumpkin and Oatmeal

5 Minutes

10 Minutes

2 servings

Ingredients:

·1/2 cup rolled oats
·1 cup water or milk (breast milk, formula, or whole milk)
·1/4 cup pumpkin puree (canned or homemade, unsweetened)
A pinch of cinnamon or nutmeg (optional)

Practical Tips for Preparing and Planning Meals:

Batch Cooking: *Prepare a larger batch of oatmeal and store it in the refrigerator. Reheat individual portions as needed.*
Quick Pumpkin Prep: *Use canned pumpkin puree for a quick and easy option. Ensure it's plain and unsweetened.*
Consistency Adjustment: *Add more water or milk to adjust the oatmeal's consistency to your baby's preference.*
Meal Variety: *Experiment with adding other baby-safe spices like a tiny pinch of ginger for added flavor.*

Storage Information:

Refrigerator: *Store the prepared oatmeal in an airtight container for up to 3 days.*
Freezer: *Portion the oatmeal into small, airtight containers or ice cube trays and freeze for up to 1 month. Thaw in the refrigerator overnight before reheating.*

Instructions:

1. **Prepare the Pumpkin:**
Make sure the canned pumpkin puree is basic and unsweetened before using it. If using fresh pumpkin, steam and puree it until smooth.
2. **Cook the Oats:**
In a small saucepan, bring the water or milk to a boil.
Add the rolled oats and reduce the heat to medium-low.
Cook the oats, stirring occasionally, for about 5-7 minutes or until they are soft and have absorbed most of the liquid.
3. **Combine and Serve:**
After taking the oats off the stove, mix in the pureed pumpkin.
Add a pinch of cinnamon or nutmeg if desired and mix well.
Allow the oatmeal to cool to a safe temperature before serving.

Nutritional Value per Serving (Approximate):
Calories: 110 Proteins: 3g Fats: 2g Carbohydrates: 22g

5 Minutes

0 Minutes

2 servings

Mango Yogurt

Ingredients:

·1/2 cup plain whole milk yogurt
1/2 cup fresh or frozen mango chunks
(thawed if frozen)

Practical Tips for Preparing and Planning Meals:

Batch Preparation: *Prepare multiple servings and store them in the refrigerator for quick access.*
Texture Variation: *For older babies, you can leave some small mango chunks for added texture.*
Flavor Variety: *Experiment with other fruits like peaches, bananas, or strawberries for different flavors.*

Storage Information:

Refrigerator: *Store the prepared mango yogurt in an airtight container for up to 2 days.*
Freezer: *While yogurt can change texture when frozen, you can freeze the mixture in small portions for up to 1 month. Thaw in the refrigerator before serving.*

Instructions:

1. **Prepare the Mango:**
If using fresh mango, peel and cut the mango into small chunks.
If using frozen mango, thaw the chunks completely.
2. **Blend the Ingredients:**
In a blender or a small food processor, combine the yogurt and mango chunks. Blend until smooth and creamy.
3. **Serve:**
Serve immediately or store as needed.

Nutritional Value per Serving (Approximate):

Calories: 90 Proteins: 4g Fats: 2g Carbohydrates: 15g

Apple and Oatmeal

Ingredients:

·1/2 cup rolled oats
·1 cup water or milk (breast milk, formula, or whole milk)
·1 small apple, peeled, cored, and finely chopped or grated
·A pinch of cinnamon (optional)

Practical Tips for Preparing and Planning Meals:

Batch Cooking: Prepare a larger batch of oatmeal and store it in the refrigerator. Reheat individual portions as needed.
Quick Apple Prep: Use a food processor to finely chop the apple quickly.
Consistency Adjustment: Add more water or milk to adjust the oatmeal's consistency to your baby's preference.
Meal Variety: Swap the apple for other baby-safe fruits like pears, peaches, or bananas to vary the flavors.

Storage Information:

Refrigerator: Store the prepared oatmeal in an airtight container for up to 3 days.
Freezer: Portion the oatmeal into small, airtight containers or ice cube trays and freeze for up to 1 month. Thaw in the refrigerator overnight before reheating.

Instructions:

1. **Prepare the Apple:**
Peel, core, and finely chop or grate the apple. Set aside.
2. **Cook the Oats:**
In a small saucepan, bring the water or milk to a boil.
Add the rolled oats and reduce the heat to medium-low.
Cook the oats, stirring occasionally, for about 5-7 minutes or until they are soft and have absorbed most of the liquid.
3. **Add the Apple:**
Add the chopped or grated apple to the saucepan.
Stir well and continue to cook for another 2-3 minutes, until the apple is soft.
If desired, add a pinch of cinnamon and mix well.
4. **Serve:**
Remove from heat and allow the oatmeal to cool to a safe temperature before serving.

Nutritional Value per Serving (Approximate):

Calories: 120 Proteins: 3g Fats: 2g Carbohydrates: 24g

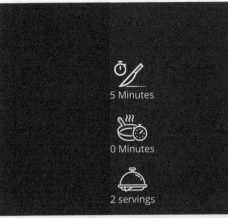

5 Minutes

0 Minutes

2 servings

Pear and Banana Mash

Ingredients:

·1 ripe pear
·1 ripe banana

Practical Tips for Preparing and Planning Meals:

Batch Preparation: Prepare multiple servings and store them in the refrigerator for quick access.
Texture Variation: For older babies, you can leave some small chunks for added texture and to help them develop chewing skills.
Flavor Variety: Experiment with adding a small pinch of cinnamon or mixing in other baby-safe fruits like apples or peaches.

Storage Information:

Refrigerator: Store the prepared pear and banana mash in an airtight container for up to 1 day. Since both fruits can brown quickly, use a little lemon juice to preserve color (use sparingly and only if your baby tolerates citrus).
Freezer: While fresh is best, you can freeze the mash in small portions for up to 1 month. Thaw in the refrigerator before serving.

Instructions:

1. **Prepare the Pear:**
Wash the pear thoroughly, peel it, and remove the core.
Chop the pear into small pieces or mash it if it's very ripe.
2. **Prepare the Banana:**
After peeling, chop the banana into large pieces.
3. **Mash and Combine:**
In a small bowl, combine the chopped pear and banana.
Use a fork or a potato masher to mash the fruits together until smooth and well combined. For younger babies, you may want to use a blender for a smoother texture.
4. **Serve:**
Serve the pear and banana mash immediately or store as needed.

Nutritional Value per Serving (Approximate):
Calories: 80 Proteins: 1g Fats: 0.5g Carbohydrates: 20g

5 Minutes

0 Minutes

2 servings

Peach and Cottage Cheese

Ingredients:

·1/2 cup cottage cheese (full-fat, small curd)
·1 ripe peach, peeled, pitted, and finely chopped or pureed

Practical Tips for Preparing and Planning Meals:

Batch Preparation: Prepare multiple servings and store them in the refrigerator for quick access.
Texture Variation: For older babies, you can leave some small peach chunks for added texture.
Flavor Variety: Experiment with other fruits like pears, apples, or berries to vary the flavors.

Storage Information:

Refrigerator: Store the prepared peach and cottage cheese mixture in an airtight container for up to 2 days.
Freezer: Cottage cheese can change texture when frozen, so it's best to serve this fresh or refrigerated.

Instructions:

1. **Prepare the Peach:**
Peel, pit, and finely chop or puree the peach. If the peach is very ripe, mashing it with a fork will suffice.
2. **Combine Ingredients:**
In a small bowl, combine the cottage cheese and the chopped or pureed peach.
Mix well until the peach is evenly distributed throughout the cottage cheese.
3. **Serve:**
Serve the peach and cottage cheese mixture immediately or store as needed.

Nutritional Value per Serving (Approximate):
Calories: 90 Proteins: 5g Fats: 2g Carbohydrates: 12g

Avocado and Blueberry Smoothie

Ingredients:

·1/2 ripe avocado
·1/2 cup fresh or frozen blueberries
(thawed if frozen)
·1/2 cup water or milk (breast milk,
formula, or whole milk)

Practical Tips for Preparing and Planning Meals:

Batch Preparation: Make a larger batch and store it in the refrigerator for quick access.
Smoothie Popsicles: Pour the smoothie into popsicle molds and freeze for a refreshing treat.
Texture Variation: For older babies, you can blend less to leave some small chunks for added texture.

Storage Information:

Refrigerator: Store the prepared smoothie in an airtight container for up to 2 days.
Freezer: Pour into ice cube trays or popsicle molds and freeze for up to 1 month. Thaw individual portions in the refrigerator before serving or enjoy as frozen treats.

Instructions:

1. **Prepare the Avocado:**
Cut the avocado in half, remove the pit, and scoop out the flesh.
2. **Combine Ingredients:**
In a blender, combine the avocado, blueberries, and water or milk.
Blend until smooth and creamy. Add more liquid if needed to achieve the desired consistency.
3. **Serve:**
Pour the smoothie into a cup and serve immediately.

Nutritional Value per Serving (Approximate):
Calories: 120 Proteins: 2g Fats: 6g Carbohydrates: 16g

5 Minutes

0 Minutes

2 servings

Strawberry and Banana Yogurt

Ingredients:

·1/2 cup plain whole milk yogurt
·1/2 ripe banana
·1/4 cup fresh or frozen strawberries
(thawed if frozen)

Practical Tips for Preparing and Planning Meals:

Batch Preparation: Prepare multiple servings and store them in the refrigerator for quick access.
Texture Variation: For older babies, you can leave some small fruit chunks for added texture.
Flavor Variety: Experiment with other fruits like blueberries, peaches, or mangoes for different flavors.

Storage Information:

Refrigerator: Store the prepared strawberry and banana yogurt in an airtight container for up to 2 days.
Freezer: While yogurt can change texture when frozen, you can freeze the mixture in small portions for up to 1 month. Thaw in the refrigerator before serving.

Instructions:

1. **Prepare the Fruits:**
Peel the banana and cut it into chunks. Wash the strawberries thoroughly and remove the stems.
2. **Blend the Ingredients:**
In a blender or a small food processor, combine the yogurt, banana, and strawberries.
Blend until smooth and creamy.
3. **Serve:**
Serve immediately or store as needed.

Nutritional Value per Serving (Approximate):

Calories: 100 Proteins: 4g Fats: 2g Carbohydrates: 18g

5 Minutes

20 Minutes

2 servings

Apple and Banana Quinoa

Ingredients:

- ·1/4 cup quinoa
- ·1/2 cup water
- ·1 small apple, peeled, cored, and finely chopped or grated
- ·1/2 ripe banana, mashed
- ·A pinch of cinnamon (optional)

Practical Tips for Preparing and Planning Meals:

Batch Cooking: Prepare a larger batch and store it in the refrigerator. Reheat individual portions as needed.
Quick Apple Prep: Use a food processor to quickly chop or grate the apple.
Consistency Adjustment: Add more water or milk to adjust the quinoa's consistency to your baby's preference.
Meal Variety: Swap the apple for other baby-safe fruits like pears or peaches to vary the flavors.

Storage Information:

Refrigerator: Store the prepared quinoa mixture in an airtight container for up to 3 days.
Freezer: Portion the quinoa mixture into small, airtight containers or ice cube trays and freeze for up to 1 month. Thaw in the refrigerator overnight before reheating.

Instructions:

1. **Prepare the Quinoa:**
Rinse the quinoa thoroughly under cold water to remove any bitterness.
2. **Cook the Quinoa:**
In a small saucepan, combine the rinsed quinoa and water.
Bring to a boil, then reduce the heat to low, cover, and simmer for about 10 minutes.
3. **Add Apple and Continue Cooking:**
Add the finely chopped or grated apple to the saucepan with the quinoa.
Stir well, cover, and continue to simmer for another 10 minutes, or until the quinoa is tender and the apple pieces are soft.
4. **Add Banana and Mix:**
After taking the saucepan off of the burner, add the mashed banana and mix.
Add a pinch of cinnamon if desired and mix well.
5. **Serve:**
Allow the mixture to cool to a safe temperature before serving.

Nutritional Value per Serving (Approximate):
Calories: 130 Proteins: 3g Fats: 2g Carbohydrates: 26g

LUNCH

5 Minutes

25 Minutes

2 servings

Sweet Potato and Carrot Puree

Ingredients:

·*1 small sweet potato, peeled and diced*
·*1 large carrot, peeled and diced*
·*1/2 cup water or vegetable broth (low sodium)*

Practical Tips for Preparing and Planning Meals:

Batch Cooking: *Prepare a larger batch and store it in the refrigerator or freezer for quick meals.*
Smooth Texture: *Ensure a smooth texture by blending thoroughly, especially for younger babies.*
Flavor Variety: *Add a pinch of mild herbs like parsley for added flavor as your baby grows accustomed to new tastes.*

Storage Information:

Refrigerator: *Store the prepared puree in an airtight container for up to 3 days.*
Freezer: *Portion the puree into small, airtight containers or ice cube trays and freeze for up to 1 month. Thaw in the refrigerator overnight before reheating.*

Instructions:

1. **Prepare the Vegetables:**
Dice and peel the sweet potato, then cut it into little pieces.
2. **Cook the Vegetables:**
In a small saucepan, combine the sweet potato, carrot, and water or vegetable broth.
Bring to a boil, then reduce the heat to low, cover, and simmer for about 20 minutes, or until the vegetables are very tender.
3. **Puree the Mixture:**
Remove the saucepan from the heat and let it cool slightly.
Transfer the cooked vegetables and any remaining liquid to a blender or use an immersion blender.
Blend until smooth. Add additional water or broth as needed to achieve the desired consistency.
4. **Serve:**
Allow the puree to cool to a safe temperature before serving.

Nutritional Value per Serving (Approximate):
Calories: 80 Proteins: 1g Fats: 0.2g Carbohydrates: 19g

5 Minutes

20 Minutes

2 servings

Spinach and Potato Puree

Ingredients:

·1 small potato, peeled and diced
·1 cup fresh spinach leaves, washed and chopped
·1/2 cup water or low-sodium vegetable broth
A pinch of nutmeg (optional)

Practical Tips for Preparing and Planning Meals:

Batch Cooking: Prepare a larger batch and store it in the refrigerator or freezer for quick meals.
Smooth Texture: Ensure a smooth texture by blending thoroughly, especially for younger babies.
Flavor Variety: Experiment with adding other baby-safe vegetables like peas or carrots for added nutrition and flavor.

Storage Information:

Refrigerator: Store the prepared puree in an airtight container for up to 3 days.
Freezer: Portion the puree into small, airtight containers or ice cube trays and freeze for up to 1 month. Thaw in the refrigerator overnight before reheating.

Instructions:

1. **Prepare the Potato:**
Peel and dice the potato into small pieces.
2. **Cook the Potato:**
In a small saucepan, combine the diced potato and water or vegetable broth.
Bring to a boil, then reduce the heat to low, cover, and simmer for about 15 minutes, or until the potato is very tender.
3. **Add the Spinach:**
Add the chopped spinach to the saucepan and cook for an additional 3-5 minutes, until the spinach is wilted and soft.
4. **Blend the Puree:**
Remove the saucepan from the heat and let it cool slightly.
Transfer the cooked potato and spinach mixture to a blender or use an immersion blender.
Blend until smooth, adding a little more water or broth if necessary to reach the desired consistency.
Add a pinch of nutmeg if desired and mix well.
5. **Serve:**
Allow the puree to cool to a safe temperature before serving.

Nutritional Value per Serving (Approximate):
Calories: 70 Proteins: 2g Fats: 0.5g Carbohydrates: 15g

5 Minutes

20 Minutes

2 servings

Carrot and Lentil Mash

Ingredients:

·1/4 cup red lentils, rinsed
·1 large carrot, peeled and diced
·1 cup water or low-sodium vegetable broth
·A pinch of cumin (optional)

Instructions:

1. **Prepare the Ingredients:**
Peel and dice the carrot.
Rinse the red lentils thoroughly under cold water.
2. **Cook the Lentils and Carrot:**
In a small saucepan, combine the lentils, diced carrot, and water or vegetable broth.
Bring to a boil, then reduce the heat to low, cover, and simmer for about 20 minutes, or until the lentils and carrots are very tender.
3. **Mash the Mixture:**
Remove the saucepan from the heat and let it cool slightly.
Use a fork or a potato masher to mash the lentils and carrots together until smooth.
For a finer texture, use an immersion blender or transfer the mixture to a blender.
Add a pinch of cumin if desired and mix well.
4. **Serve:**
Allow the mash to cool to a safe temperature before serving.

Practical Tips for Preparing and Planning Meals:

Batch Cooking: Prepare a larger batch and store it in the refrigerator or freezer for quick meals.
Smooth Texture: Ensure a smooth texture by blending thoroughly, especially for younger babies.
Flavor Variety: Experiment with adding other baby-safe vegetables like sweet potatoes or peas for added nutrition and flavor.

Storage Information:

Refrigerator: Store the prepared mash in an airtight container for up to 3 days.
Freezer: Portion the mash into small, airtight containers or ice cube trays and freeze for up to 1 month. Thaw in the refrigerator overnight before reheating.

Nutritional Value per Serving (Approximate):

Calories: 90 Proteins: 5g Fats: 0.5g Carbohydrates: 18g

5 Minutes

20 Minutes

2 servings

Zucchini and Potato Puree

Ingredients:

·1 small potato, peeled and diced
·1 small zucchini, diced
·1/2 cup water or low-sodium vegetable broth

Practical Tips for Preparing and Planning Meals:

Batch Cooking: Prepare a larger batch and store it in the refrigerator or freezer for quick meals.
Smooth Texture: Ensure a smooth texture by blending thoroughly, especially for younger babies.
Flavor Variety: Experiment with adding other baby-safe vegetables like carrots or peas for added nutrition and flavor.

Storage Information:

Refrigerator: Store the prepared puree in an airtight container for up to 3 days.
Freezer: Portion the puree into small, airtight containers or ice cube trays and freeze for up to 1 month. Thaw in the refrigerator overnight before reheating.

Instructions:

1. **Prepare the Vegetables:**
Chop and peel the potato.
Wash and dice the zucchini.
2. **Cook the Vegetables:**
In a small saucepan, combine the diced potato, zucchini, and water or vegetable broth.
Bring to a boil, then reduce the heat to low, cover, and simmer for about 15-20 minutes, or until the vegetables are very tender.
3. **Blend the Puree:**
Remove the saucepan from the heat and let it cool slightly.
Use an immersion blender to puree the mixture until smooth. Alternatively, transfer the cooked vegetables and any remaining liquid to a blender and blend until smooth. If necessary, add more water or broth to reach the desired consistency.
4. **Serve:**
Allow the puree to cool to a safe temperature before serving.

Nutritional Value per Serving (Approximate):
Calories: 70 Proteins: 1.5g Fats: 0.5g Carbohydrates: 15g

5 Minutes

15 Minutes

2 servings

Broccoli and Cheese Puree

Ingredients:

·1 cup broccoli florets
·1 small potato, peeled and diced
·1/2 cup water or low-sodium vegetable broth
1/4 cup shredded mild cheddar cheese

Practical Tips for Preparing and Planning Meals:

Batch Cooking: Prepare a larger batch and store it in the refrigerator or freezer for quick meals.
Smooth Texture: Ensure a smooth texture by blending thoroughly, especially for younger babies.
Flavor Variety: Experiment with adding other baby-safe vegetables like peas or carrots for added nutrition and flavor.

Storage Information:

Refrigerator: Store the prepared puree in an airtight container for up to 3 days.
Freezer: Portion the puree into small, airtight containers or ice cube trays and freeze for up to 1 month. Thaw in the refrigerator overnight before reheating.

Instructions:

1. **Prepare the Vegetables:**
Wash and cut the broccoli into small florets. Peel and dice the potato.
2. **Cook the Vegetables:**
In a small saucepan, combine the broccoli florets, diced potato, and water or vegetable broth.
Bring to a boil, then reduce the heat to low, cover, and simmer for about 10-15 minutes, or until the vegetables are very tender.
3. **Blend the Puree:**
Remove the saucepan from the heat and let it cool slightly.
Use an immersion blender to puree the mixture until smooth. Alternatively, transfer the cooked vegetables and any remaining liquid to a blender and blend until smooth.
Once the cheese has completely melted and incorporated, add the shredded cheddar and combine once more.
If necessary, add more water or broth to reach the desired consistency.
4. **Serve:**
Allow the puree to cool to a safe temperature before serving.

Nutritional Value per Serving (Approximate):
Calories: 80 Proteins: 5g Fats: 3g Carbohydrates: 10g

5 Minutes

10 Minutes

2 servings

Pea and Mint Puree

Ingredients:

·1 cup fresh or frozen peas
·1/4 cup water or low-sodium vegetable broth
·3-4 fresh mint leaves, finely chopped

Practical Tips for Preparing and Planning Meals:

Batch Cooking: Prepare a larger batch and store it in the refrigerator or freezer for quick meals.
Smooth Texture: Ensure a smooth texture by blending thoroughly, especially for younger babies.
Flavor Variety: Experiment with adding other baby-safe herbs like parsley or basil for different flavors.

Storage Information:

Refrigerator: Store the prepared puree in an airtight container for up to 3 days.
Freezer: Portion the puree into small, airtight containers or ice cube trays and freeze for up to 1 month. Thaw in the refrigerator overnight before reheating.

Instructions:

1. **Cook the Peas:**
If using fresh peas, shell them. If using frozen peas, there is no need to thaw them.
In a small saucepan, combine the peas and water or vegetable broth.
Bring to a boil, then reduce the heat to low, cover, and simmer for about 5-7 minutes, or until the peas are tender.
2. **Add Mint and Blend:**
Add the finely chopped mint leaves to the saucepan.
Use an immersion blender to puree the mixture until smooth. Alternatively, transfer the cooked peas and mint along with any remaining liquid to a blender and blend until smooth.
If necessary, add more water or broth to reach the desired consistency.
3. **Serve:**
Allow the puree to cool to a safe temperature before serving.

Nutritional Value per Serving (Approximate):
Calories: 60 Proteins: 3g Fats: 0.5g Carbohydrates: 10g

10 Minutes

20 Minutes

2 servings

Chickpea and Carrot Puree

Ingredients:

·*1/2 cup cooked chickpeas (canned, rinsed, and drained, or home-cooked)*
·*1 large carrot, peeled and diced*
·*1/2 cup water or low-sodium vegetable broth*
·*A pinch of cumin (optional)*

Practical Tips for Preparing and Planning Meals:

Batch Cooking: *Prepare a larger batch and store it in the refrigerator or freezer for quick meals.*
Smooth Texture: *Ensure a smooth texture by blending thoroughly, especially for younger babies.*
Flavor Variety: *Experiment with adding other baby-safe spices like a tiny pinch of cinnamon or mild herbs like parsley for different flavors.*

Storage Information:

Refrigerator: *Store the prepared puree in an airtight container for up to 3 days.*
Freezer: *Portion the puree into small, airtight containers or ice cube trays and freeze for up to 1 month. Thaw in the refrigerator overnight before reheating.*

Instructions:

1. **Prepare the Ingredients:**
Peel and dice the carrot.
If using canned chickpeas, rinse and drain them well.
2. **Cook the Carrot:**
In a small saucepan, combine the diced carrot and water or vegetable broth.
Bring to a boil, then reduce the heat to low, cover, and simmer for about 15 minutes, or until the carrot is very tender.
3. **Add Chickpeas and Blend:**
Add the cooked chickpeas to the saucepan with the carrots.
Continue to cook for an additional 5 minutes to heat the chickpeas through. Remove the saucepan from the heat and let it cool slightly.
Use an immersion blender to puree the mixture until smooth. Alternatively, transfer the cooked chickpeas and carrots along with any remaining liquid to a blender and blend until smooth.
Add a pinch of cumin if desired and mix well.
4. **Serve:**
Allow the puree to cool to a safe temperature before serving.

Nutritional Value per Serving (Approximate):
Calories: 80 Proteins: 3g Fats: 1g Carbohydrates: 15g

Sweet Potato and Green Bean Puree

Ingredients:

·1 small sweet potato, peeled and diced
·1/2 cup green beans, trimmed and chopped
·1/2 cup water or low-sodium vegetable broth

Practical Tips for Preparing and Planning Meals:

Batch Cooking: Prepare a larger batch and store it in the refrigerator or freezer for quick meals.
Smooth Texture: Ensure a smooth texture by blending thoroughly, especially for younger babies.
Flavor Variety: Experiment with adding other baby-safe vegetables like carrots or peas for added nutrition and flavor.

Storage Information:

Refrigerator: Store the prepared puree in an airtight container for up to 3 days.
Freezer: Portion the puree into small, airtight containers or ice cube trays and freeze for up to 1 month. Thaw in the refrigerator overnight before reheating.

Instructions:

1. **Prepare the Vegetables:**
Peel and dice the sweet potato.
Trim and chop the green beans.
2. **Cook the Vegetables:**
In a small saucepan, combine the diced sweet potato, green beans, and water or vegetable broth.
Bring to a boil, then reduce the heat to low, cover, and simmer for about 15-20 minutes, or until the vegetables are very tender.
3. **Blend the Puree:**
Remove the saucepan from the heat and let it cool slightly.
Use an immersion blender to puree the mixture until smooth. Alternatively, transfer the cooked vegetables and any remaining liquid to a blender and blend until smooth. If necessary, add more water or broth to reach the desired consistency.
4. **Serve:**
Allow the puree to cool to a safe temperature before serving.

Nutritional Value per Serving (Approximate):
Calories: 70 Proteins: 2g Fats: 0.2g Carbohydrates: 16g

10 Minutes

30 Minutes

2 servings

Beef, Broccoli, and Potato Puree

Ingredients:

- 1/4 cup lean ground beef
- 1 small potato, peeled and diced
- 1/2 cup broccoli florets, chopped
- 1 cup water or low-sodium vegetable broth

Practical Tips for Preparing and Planning Meals:

Batch Cooking: Prepare a larger batch and store it in the refrigerator or freezer for quick meals.
Smooth Texture: Ensure a smooth texture by blending thoroughly, especially for younger babies.
Flavor Variety: Experiment with adding other baby-safe vegetables like carrots or peas for added nutrition and flavor.

Storage Information:

Refrigerator: Store the prepared puree in an airtight container for up to 3 days.
Freezer: Portion the puree into small, airtight containers or ice cube trays and freeze for up to 1 month. Thaw in the refrigerator overnight before reheating.

Instructions:

1. **Prepare the Ingredients:**
Peel and dice the potato.
Wash and chop the broccoli into small florets.
2. **Cook the Beef:**
In a small saucepan, cook the ground beef over medium heat until fully cooked, breaking it into small pieces as it cooks. Drain any excess fat if necessary.
3. **Cook the Vegetables:**
Add the diced potato, broccoli florets, and water or vegetable broth to the saucepan with the cooked beef.
Bring to a boil, then reduce the heat to low, cover, and simmer for about 20 minutes, or until the vegetables are very tender.
4. **Blend the Puree:**
Remove the saucepan from the heat and let it cool slightly.
Use an immersion blender to puree the mixture until smooth. Alternatively, transfer the cooked mixture and any remaining liquid to a blender and blend until smooth. If necessary, add more water or broth to reach the desired consistency.
5. **Serve:**
Allow the puree to cool to a safe temperature before serving.

Nutritional Value per Serving (Approximate):
Calories: 120 Proteins: 8g Fats: 3g Carbohydrates: 15g

Zucchini and Lentil Mash

Ingredients:

·1/4 cup red lentils, rinsed
·1 small zucchini, diced
·1 small carrot, peeled and diced
·1/2 small onion, finely chopped
·1 cup water or low-sodium vegetable broth

Practical Tips for Preparing and Planning Meals:

Batch Cooking: Prepare a larger batch and store it in the refrigerator or freezer for quick meals.
Smooth Texture: Ensure a smooth texture by mashing thoroughly, especially for younger babies.
Flavor Variety: Experiment with adding other baby-safe vegetables like sweet potatoes or peas for added nutrition and flavor.

Storage Information:

Refrigerator: Store the prepared mash in an airtight container for up to 3 days.
Freezer: Portion the mash into small, airtight containers or ice cube trays and freeze for up to 1 month. Thaw in the refrigerator overnight before reheating.

Instructions:

1. **Prepare the Ingredients:**
Rinse the red lentils thoroughly under cold water.
Dice the zucchini.
Peel and dice the carrot.
Finely chop the onion.
2. **Cook the Lentils and Vegetables:**
In a small saucepan, combine the rinsed lentils, diced zucchini, diced carrot, chopped onion, and water or vegetable broth.
Bring to a boil, then reduce the heat to low, cover, and simmer for about 20 minutes, or until the lentils and vegetables are very tender.
3. **Mash the Mixture:**
Remove the saucepan from the heat and let it cool slightly.
Use a fork or a potato masher to mash the lentils and vegetables together until smooth. For a finer texture, use an immersion blender or transfer the mixture to a blender and blend until smooth.
If necessary, add more water or broth to reach the desired consistency.
4. **Serve:**
Allow the mash to cool to a safe temperature before serving.

Nutritional Value per Serving (Approximate):
Calories: 90 Proteins: 5g Fats: 0.5g Carbohydrates: 16g

Pea and Carrot Puree

Ingredients:

- 1 cup fresh or frozen peas
- 1 large carrot, peeled and diced
- 1/2 cup water or low-sodium vegetable broth

Practical Tips for Preparing and Planning Meals:

Batch Cooking: Prepare a larger batch and store it in the refrigerator or freezer for quick meals.
Smooth Texture: Ensure a smooth texture by blending thoroughly, especially for younger babies.
Flavor Variety: Experiment with adding other baby-safe vegetables like sweet potatoes or spinach for added nutrition and flavor.

Storage Information:

Refrigerator: Store the prepared puree in an airtight container for up to 3 days.
Freezer: Portion the puree into small, airtight containers or ice cube trays and freeze for up to 1 month. Thaw in the refrigerator overnight before reheating.

Instructions:

1. **Prepare the Vegetables:**
Peel and dice the carrot.
If using fresh peas, wash them. If using frozen peas, there is no need to thaw them.
2. **Cook the Vegetables:**
In a small saucepan, combine the diced carrot and water or vegetable broth.
Bring to a boil, then reduce the heat to low, cover, and simmer for about 10 minutes, or until the carrot is tender.
Add the peas and cook for an additional 5 minutes, or until the peas are tender.
3. **Blend the Puree:**
Remove the saucepan from the heat and let it cool slightly.
Use an immersion blender to puree the mixture until smooth. Alternatively, transfer the cooked vegetables and any remaining liquid to a blender and blend until smooth.
If necessary, add more water or broth to reach the desired consistency.
4. **Serve:**
Allow the puree to cool to a safe temperature before serving.

Nutritional Value per Serving (Approximate):
Calories: 60 Proteins: 2g Fats: 0.2g Carbohydrates: 13g

Sweet Potato and Pea Puree

Ingredients:

·1 small sweet potato, peeled and diced
·1/2 cup fresh or frozen peas
·1/2 cup water or low-sodium vegetable broth

Practical Tips for Preparing and Planning Meals:

Batch Cooking: Prepare a larger batch and store it in the refrigerator or freezer for quick meals.
Smooth Texture: Ensure a smooth texture by blending thoroughly, especially for younger babies.
Flavor Variety: Experiment with adding other baby-safe vegetables like carrots or spinach for added nutrition and flavor.

Storage Information:

Refrigerator: Store the prepared puree in an airtight container for up to 3 days.
Freezer: Portion the puree into small, airtight containers or ice cube trays and freeze for up to 1 month. Thaw in the refrigerator overnight before reheating.

Instructions:

1. **Prepare the Vegetables:**
Peel and dice the sweet potato.
If using fresh peas, wash them. If using frozen peas, there is no need to thaw them.
2. **Cook the Sweet Potato:**
In a small saucepan, combine the diced sweet potato and water or vegetable broth.
Bring to a boil, then reduce the heat to low, cover, and simmer for about 10 minutes, or until the sweet potato is tender.
3. **Add the Peas:**
Add the peas to the saucepan with the sweet potato and cook for an additional 5 minutes, or until the peas are tender.
4. **Blend the Puree:**
Remove the saucepan from the heat and let it cool slightly.
Use an immersion blender to puree the mixture until smooth. Alternatively, transfer the cooked vegetables and any remaining liquid to a blender and blend until smooth. If necessary, add more water or broth to reach the desired consistency.
5. **Serve:**
Allow the puree to cool to a safe temperature before serving.

Nutritional Value per Serving (Approximate):
Calories: 70 Proteins: 2g Fats: 0.2g Carbohydrates: 16g

DINNER

10 Minutes

20 Minutes

2 servings

Chicken and Broccoli Mash

Ingredients:

·1/4 cup boneless, skinless chicken breast, diced
·1 cup broccoli florets, chopped
·1 small potato, peeled and diced
·1 cup water or low-sodium vegetable broth

Practical Tips for Preparing and Planning Meals:

Batch Cooking: Prepare a larger batch and store it in the refrigerator or freezer for quick meals.
Smooth Texture: Ensure a smooth texture by mashing thoroughly, especially for younger babies.
Flavor Variety: Experiment with adding other baby-safe vegetables like peas or carrots for added nutrition and flavor.

Storage Information:

Refrigerator: Store the prepared mash in an airtight container for up to 3 days.
Freezer: Portion the mash into small, airtight containers or ice cube trays and freeze for up to 1 month. Thaw in the refrigerator overnight before reheating.

Instructions:

1. **Prepare the Ingredients:**
Peel and dice the potato.
Wash and chop the broccoli into small florets.
Dice the chicken breast into small pieces.
2. **Cook the Chicken and Vegetables:**
In a small saucepan, combine the diced chicken, potato, broccoli, and water or vegetable broth.
Bring to a boil, then reduce the heat to low, cover, and simmer for about 20 minutes, or until the chicken is cooked through and the vegetables are very tender.
3. **Mash the Mixture:**
Remove the saucepan from the heat and let it cool slightly.
Use a fork or a potato masher to mash the chicken, potato, and broccoli together until smooth. For a finer texture, use an immersion blender or transfer the mixture to a blender and blend until smooth.
If necessary, add more water or broth to reach the desired consistency.
4. **Serve:**
Allow the mash to cool to a safe temperature before serving.

Nutritional Value per Serving (Approximate):
Calories: 80 Proteins: 8g Fats: 3g Carbohydrates: 5g

Mashed Peas and Brown Rice Blend

Ingredients:

- ·1/2 cup fresh or frozen peas
- ·1/4 cup brown rice
- ·1 cup water or low-sodium vegetable broth

Practical Tips for Preparing and Planning Meals:

Batch Cooking: Prepare a larger batch of the blend and store it in the refrigerator or freezer for quick meals.
Smooth Texture: Ensure a smooth texture by blending thoroughly, especially for younger babies.
Flavor Variety: Experiment with adding other baby-safe vegetables like carrots or sweet potatoes for added nutrition and flavor.

Storage Information:

Refrigerator: Store the prepared blend in an airtight container for up to 3 days.
Freezer: Portion the blend into small, airtight containers or ice cube trays and freeze for up to 1 month. Thaw in the refrigerator overnight before reheating.

Instructions:

1. **Cook the Brown Rice:**
Rinse the brown rice under cold water.
In a small saucepan, combine the rinsed brown rice and water or vegetable broth.
Bring to a boil, then reduce the heat to low, cover, and simmer for about 20 minutes, or until the rice is tender and has absorbed most of the liquid.
2. **Cook the Peas:**
In case of using fresh peas, wash them. If using frozen peas, there is no need to thaw them.
In a separate small saucepan, bring water to a boil.
Add the peas and cook for about 5 minutes, or until tender.
3. **Blend the Peas and Rice:**
Combine the cooked peas and brown rice in a blender or food processor.
Blend until smooth, adding a little more water or broth if necessary to achieve the desired consistency.
4. **Serve:**
Allow the blend to cool to a safe temperature before serving.

Nutritional Value per Serving (Approximate):
Calories: 90 Proteins: 3g Fats: 0.5g Carbohydrates: 20g

10 Minutes

20 Minutes

2 servings

Salmon and Sweet Potato Mash

Ingredients:

·1 small sweet potato, peeled and diced
·2 ounces fresh salmon fillet, boneless and skinless
·1/2 cup water or low-sodium vegetable broth
·A pinch of mild herbs like dill or parsley (optional)

Practical Tips for Preparing and Planning Meals:

Batch Cooking: Prepare a larger batch and store it in the refrigerator or freezer for quick meals.
Smooth Texture: Ensure a smooth texture by mashing or blending thoroughly, especially for younger babies.
Flavor Variety: Experiment with adding other baby-safe vegetables like peas or carrots for added nutrition and flavor.

Storage Information:

Refrigerator: Store the prepared mash in an airtight container for up to 2 days.
Freezer: Portion the mash into small, airtight containers or ice cube trays and freeze for up to 1 month. Thaw in the refrigerator overnight before reheating.

Instructions:

1. **Prepare the Sweet Potato:**
Peel and dice the sweet potato into small cubes.
2. **Cook the Sweet Potato:**
In a small saucepan, combine the diced sweet potato and water or vegetable broth. Bring to a boil, then reduce the heat to low, cover, and simmer for about 10-15 minutes, or until the sweet potato is tender.
3. **Cook the Salmon:**
While the sweet potato is cooking, place the salmon fillet in a steamer basket over boiling water.
Cover and steam for about 5-7 minutes, or until the salmon is cooked through and flakes easily with a fork.
4. **Mash the Mixture:**
Once the sweet potato is tender, remove the saucepan from the heat and let it cool slightly.
Add the cooked salmon to the saucepan with the sweet potato.
Use a fork or a potato masher to mash the sweet potato and salmon together until smooth. For a finer texture, use an immersion blender or transfer the mixture to a blender and blend until smooth.
If desired, add a pinch of mild herbs like dill or parsley and mix well.
If necessary, add more water or broth to reach the desired consistency.
5. **Serve:**
Allow the mash to cool to a safe temperature before serving.

Nutritional Value per Serving (Approximate):
Calories: 110 Proteins: 7g Fats: 4g Carbohydrates: 12g

5 Minutes

20 Minutes

2 servings

Turkey and Avocado Puree

Ingredients:

·2 ounces ground turkey breast
·1 small ripe avocado
·1/2 small potato, peeled and diced
·1/2 cup water or low-sodium vegetable broth

Practical Tips for Preparing and Planning Meals:

Batch Cooking: Prepare a larger batch and store it in the refrigerator or freezer for quick meals.
Smooth Texture: Ensure a smooth texture by blending thoroughly, especially for younger babies.
Flavor Variety: Experiment with adding other baby-safe vegetables like peas or carrots for added nutrition and flavor.

Storage Information:

Refrigerator: Store the prepared puree in an airtight container for up to 2 days.
Freezer: Portion the puree into small, airtight containers or ice cube trays and freeze for up to 1 month. Thaw in the refrigerator overnight before reheating.

Instructions:

1. **Cook the Turkey:**
In a small saucepan, add the ground turkey breast and water or vegetable broth.
Bring to a boil, then reduce the heat to low, cover, and simmer for about 10 minutes, or until the turkey is fully cooked.
2. **Prepare the Potato:**
Peel and dice the potato.
Add the diced potato to the saucepan with the turkey and cook for an additional 10 minutes, or until the potato is tender.
3. **Prepare the Avocado:**
While the turkey and potato are cooking, cut the avocado in half, remove the pit, and scoop out the flesh into a small bowl.
4. **Combine and Blend:**
Once the turkey and potato are cooked and tender, remove the saucepan from the heat and let it cool slightly.
Add the cooked turkey, potato, and avocado to a blender or use an immersion blender. Blend until smooth. If necessary, add more water or broth to reach the desired consistency.
5. **Serve:**
Allow the puree to cool to a safe temperature before serving.

Nutritional Value per Serving (Approximate):
Calories: 100 Proteins: 7g Fats: 5g Carbohydrates: 5g

10 Minutes

20 Minutes

2 servings

Chicken and Apple Mash

Ingredients:

· 1/4 cup boneless, skinless chicken breast, diced
· 1 small apple, peeled, cored, and chopped
· 1 small potato, peeled and diced
· 1/2 cup water or low-sodium vegetable broth

Practical Tips for Preparing and Planning Meals:

Batch Cooking: Prepare a larger batch and store it in the refrigerator or freezer for quick meals.
Smooth Texture: Ensure a smooth texture by mashing or blending thoroughly, especially for younger babies.
Flavor Variety: Experiment with adding other baby-safe vegetables like carrots or peas for added nutrition and flavor.

Storage Information:

Refrigerator: Store the prepared mash in an airtight container for up to 2 days.
Freezer: Portion the mash into small, airtight containers or ice cube trays and freeze for up to 1 month. Thaw in the refrigerator overnight before reheating.

Instructions:

1. **Prepare the Ingredients:**
Peel, core, and chop the apple.
Peel and dice the potato.
Dice the chicken breast into small pieces.
2. **Cook the Chicken and Vegetables:**
In a small saucepan, combine the diced chicken, apple, potato, and water or vegetable broth.
Bring to a boil, then reduce the heat to low, cover, and simmer for about 20 minutes, or until the chicken is cooked through and the vegetables are very tender.
3. **Mash the Mixture:**
Remove the saucepan from the heat and let it cool slightly.
Use a fork or a potato masher to mash the chicken, apple, and potato together until smooth. For a finer texture, use an immersion blender or transfer the mixture to a blender and blend until smooth.
If necessary, add more water or broth to reach the desired consistency.
4. **Serve:**
Allow the mash to cool to a safe temperature before serving.

Nutritional Value per Serving (Approximate):
Calories: 90 Proteins: 7g Fats: 2g Carbohydrates: 10g

10 Minutes

25 Minutes

2 servings

Beef and Carrot Mash

Ingredients:

·1/4 cup lean ground beef
·1 large carrot, peeled and diced
·1 small potato, peeled and diced
·1/2 cup water or low-sodium vegetable broth

Practical Tips for Preparing and Planning Meals:

Batch Cooking: Prepare a larger batch and store it in the refrigerator or freezer for quick meals.
Smooth Texture: Ensure a smooth texture by mashing or blending thoroughly, especially for younger babies.
Flavor Variety: Experiment with adding other baby-safe vegetables like peas or sweet potatoes for added nutrition and flavor.

Storage Information:

Refrigerator: Store the prepared mash in an airtight container for up to 3 days.
Freezer: Portion the mash into small, airtight containers or ice cube trays and freeze for up to 1 month. Thaw in the refrigerator overnight before reheating.

Instructions:

1. **Prepare the Ingredients:**
Peel and dice the carrot and potato.
2. **Cook the Beef:**
In a small saucepan, add the ground beef and cook over medium heat until fully cooked, breaking it into small pieces as it cooks.
Drain any excess fat if necessary.
3. **Cook the Vegetables:**
Add the diced carrot, potato, and water or vegetable broth to the saucepan with the cooked beef.
Bring to a boil, then reduce the heat to low, cover, and simmer for about 20 minutes, or until the vegetables are very tender.
4. **Mash the Mixture:**
Remove the saucepan from the heat and let it cool slightly.
Use a fork or a potato masher to mash the beef, carrot, and potato together until smooth. For a finer texture, use an immersion blender or transfer the mixture to a blender and blend until smooth.
If necessary, add more water or broth to reach the desired consistency.
5. **Serve:**
Allow the mash to cool to a safe temperature before serving.

Nutritional Value per Serving (Approximate):
Calories: 100 Proteins: 8g Fats: 3g Carbohydrates: 10g

10 Minutes

20 Minutes

2 servings

Turkey and Sweet Potato Mash

Ingredients:

·1/4 cup ground turkey breast
·1 small sweet potato, peeled and diced
·1/2 small apple, peeled, cored, and chopped (optional for added sweetness)
·1/2 cup water or low-sodium vegetable broth

Practical Tips for Preparing and Planning Meals:

Batch Cooking: Prepare a larger batch and store it in the refrigerator or freezer for quick meals.
Smooth Texture: Ensure a smooth texture by mashing or blending thoroughly, especially for younger babies.
Flavor Variety: Experiment with adding other baby-safe vegetables like carrots or peas for added nutrition and flavor.

Storage Information:

Refrigerator: Store the prepared mash in an airtight container for up to 2 days.
Freezer: Portion the mash into small, airtight containers or ice cube trays and freeze for up to 1 month. Thaw in the refrigerator overnight before reheating.

Instructions:

1. **Prepare the Ingredients:**
Peel and dice the sweet potato.
If using, peel, core, and chop the apple.
2. **Cook the Turkey:**
In a small saucepan, add the ground turkey and cook over medium heat until fully cooked, breaking it into small pieces as it cooks.
Drain any excess fat if necessary.
3. **Cook the Vegetables:**
Add the diced sweet potato, apple (if using), and water or vegetable broth to the saucepan with the cooked turkey.
Bring to a boil, then reduce the heat to low, cover, and simmer for about 15-20 minutes, or until the sweet potato is very tender.
4. **Mash the Mixture:**
Remove the saucepan from the heat and let it cool slightly.
Use a fork or a potato masher to mash the turkey, sweet potato, and apple together until smooth. For a finer texture, use an immersion blender or transfer the mixture to a blender and blend until smooth.
If necessary, add more water or broth to reach the desired consistency.
5. **Serve:**
Allow the mash to cool to a safe temperature before serving.

Nutritional Value per Serving (Approximate):

Calories: 90 Proteins: 7g Fats: 2g Carbohydrates: 12g

10 Minutes

20 Minutes

2 servings

Chicken and Cauliflower Mash

Ingredients:

·1/4 cup boneless, skinless chicken breast, diced
·1 cup cauliflower florets, chopped
·1 small potato, peeled and diced (optional for added texture)
·1/2 cup water or low-sodium vegetable broth

Practical Tips for Preparing and Planning Meals:

Batch Cooking: Prepare a larger batch and store it in the refrigerator or freezer for quick meals.
Smooth Texture: Ensure a smooth texture by mashing or blending thoroughly, especially for younger babies.
Flavor Variety: Experiment with adding other baby-safe vegetables like carrots or peas for added nutrition and flavor.

Storage Information:

Refrigerator: Store the prepared mash in an airtight container for up to 2 days.
Freezer: Portion the mash into small, airtight containers or ice cube trays and freeze for up to 1 month. Thaw in the refrigerator overnight before reheating.

Instructions:

1. **Prepare the Ingredients:**
Peel and dice the potato (if using).
Wash and chop the cauliflower into small florets.
Dice the chicken breast into small pieces.
2. **Cook the Chicken and Vegetables:**
In a small saucepan, add the diced chicken, cauliflower, potato (if using), and water or vegetable broth.
Bring to a boil, then reduce the heat to low, cover, and simmer for about 20 minutes, or until the chicken is cooked through and the vegetables are very tender.
3. **Mash the Mixture:**
Remove the saucepan from the heat and let it cool slightly.
Use a fork or a potato masher to mash the chicken, cauliflower, and potato together until smooth. For a finer texture, use an immersion blender or transfer the mixture to a blender and blend until smooth.
If necessary, add more water or broth to reach the desired consistency.
4. **Serve:**
Allow the mash to cool to a safe temperature before serving.

Nutritional Value per Serving (Approximate):
Calories: 80 Proteins: 7g Fats: 2g Carbohydrates: 7g

10 Minutes

15 Minutes

2 servings

Salmon and Spinach Mash

Ingredients:

·2 ounces fresh salmon fillet, boneless and skinless
·1 cup fresh spinach leaves, washed and chopped
·1 small potato, peeled and diced (optional for added texture)
·1/2 cup water or low-sodium vegetable broth

Practical Tips for Preparing and Planning Meals:

Batch Cooking: Prepare a larger batch and store it in the refrigerator or freezer for quick meals.
Smooth Texture: Ensure a smooth texture by mashing or blending thoroughly, especially for younger babies.
Flavor Variety: Experiment with adding other baby-safe vegetables like peas or carrots for added nutrition and flavor.

Storage Information:

Refrigerator: Store the prepared mash in an airtight container for up to 2 days.
Freezer: Portion the mash into small, airtight containers or ice cube trays and freeze for up to 1 month. Thaw in the refrigerator overnight before reheating.

Instructions:

1. **Prepare the Ingredients:**
Peel and dice the potato (if using).
Wash and chop the spinach leaves.
Cut the salmon fillet into small pieces.
2. **Cook the Salmon:**
In a small saucepan, add the salmon and water or vegetable broth.
Bring to a boil, then reduce the heat to low, cover, and simmer for about 5-7 minutes, or until the salmon is cooked through and flakes easily with a fork.
3. **Cook the Vegetables:**
Add the diced potato (if using) to the saucepan and cook for about 10 minutes, or until the potato is tender.
Add the chopped spinach to the saucepan and cook for an additional 2-3 minutes, until the spinach is wilted and soft.
4. **Mash the Mixture:**
Remove the saucepan from the heat and let it cool slightly.
Use a fork or a potato masher to mash the salmon, spinach, and potato together until smooth. For a finer texture, use an immersion blender or transfer the mixture to a blender and blend until smooth.
If necessary, add more water or broth to reach the desired consistency.
5. **Serve:**
Allow the mash to cool to a safe temperature before serving.

Nutritional Value per Serving (Approximate):

Calories: 110 Proteins: 8g Fats: 6g Carbohydrates: 4g

10 Minutes

20 Minutes

2 servings

Turkey and Spinach Mash

Ingredients:

·1/4 cup ground turkey breast
·1 cup fresh spinach leaves, washed and chopped
·1 small potato, peeled and diced (optional for added texture)
·1/2 cup water or low-sodium vegetable broth

Practical Tips for Preparing and Planning Meals:

Batch Cooking: Prepare a larger batch and store it in the refrigerator or freezer for quick meals.
Smooth Texture: Ensure a smooth texture by mashing or blending thoroughly, especially for younger babies.
Flavor Variety: Experiment with adding other baby-safe vegetables like peas or carrots for added nutrition and flavor.

Storage Information:

Refrigerator: Store the prepared mash in an airtight container for up to 2 days.
Freezer: Portion the mash into small, airtight containers or ice cube trays and freeze for up to 1 month. Thaw in the refrigerator overnight before reheating.

Instructions:

1. **Prepare the Ingredients:**
Peel and dice the potato (if using).
Wash and chop the spinach leaves.
2. **Cook the Turkey:**
In a small saucepan, add the ground turkey and cook over medium heat until fully cooked, breaking it into small pieces as it cooks.
Drain any excess fat if necessary.
3. **Cook the Vegetables:**
Add the diced potato (if using) and water or vegetable broth to the saucepan with the cooked turkey.
Bring to a boil, then reduce the heat to low, cover, and simmer for about 15 minutes, or until the potato is tender.
Add the chopped spinach to the saucepan and cook for an additional 3-5 minutes, until the spinach is wilted and soft.
4. **Mash the Mixture:**
Remove the saucepan from the heat and let it cool slightly.
Use a fork or a potato masher to mash the turkey, spinach, and potato together until smooth. For a finer texture, use an immersion blender or transfer the mixture to a blender and blend until smooth.
If necessary, add more water or broth to reach the desired consistency.
5. **Serve:**
Allow the mash to cool to a safe temperature before serving.

Nutritional Value per Serving (Approximate):
Calories: 90 Proteins: 8g Fats: 2g Carbohydrates: 8g

10 Minutes

30 Minutes

2 servings

Rabbit, Quinoa, and Pumpkin Puree

Ingredients:

- 1/4 cup rabbit meat, diced (boneless and skinless)
- 1/4 cup quinoa, rinsed
- 1/2 cup pumpkin puree (canned or fresh)
- 1 cup water or low-sodium vegetable broth

Practical Tips for Preparing and Planning Meals:

Batch Cooking: Prepare a larger batch and store it in the refrigerator or freezer for quick meals.
Smooth Texture: Ensure a smooth texture by blending thoroughly, especially for younger babies.
Flavor Variety: Experiment with adding other baby-safe vegetables like carrots or peas for added nutrition and flavor.

Storage Information:

Refrigerator: Store the prepared puree in an airtight container for up to 3 days.
Freezer: Portion the puree into small, airtight containers or ice cube trays and freeze for up to 1 month. Thaw in the refrigerator overnight before reheating.

Instructions:

1. **Prepare the Ingredients:**
If using fresh pumpkin, peel, remove seeds, and dice it. If using canned pumpkin puree, ensure it is plain and unsweetened.
2. **Cook the Rabbit:**
In a small saucepan, add the diced rabbit meat and water or vegetable broth.
Bring to a boil, then reduce the heat to low, cover, and simmer for about 20 minutes, or until the rabbit is cooked through and tender.
3. **Cook the Quinoa:**
While the rabbit is cooking, rinse the quinoa thoroughly under cold water.
In another small saucepan, combine the quinoa with 1/2 cup of water.
Bring to a boil, then reduce the heat to low, cover, and simmer for about 15 minutes, or until the quinoa is tender and has absorbed most of the liquid.
4. **Cook the Pumpkin:**
If using fresh pumpkin, steam or boil the pumpkin until tender, about 10 minutes. In case of using canned pumpkin puree, skip this step.
5. **Combine and Blend:**
Once all ingredients are cooked, combine the rabbit, quinoa, and pumpkin in a blender or use an immersion blender.
Blend until smooth, adding more water or broth if necessary to achieve the desired consistency.
6. **Serve:**
Allow the puree to cool to a safe temperature before serving.

Nutritional Value per Serving (Approximate):
Calories: 100 Proteins: 8g Fats: 2g Carbohydrates: 12g

10 Minutes

30 Minutes

2 servings

Rabbit and Vegetable Puree

Ingredients:

· 1/4 cup rabbit meat, diced (boneless and skinless)
· 1 small carrot, peeled and diced
· 1 small potato, peeled and diced
· 1/2 cup broccoli florets, chopped
· 1/2 small zucchini, diced
· 1 cup water or low-sodium vegetable broth

Practical Tips for Preparing and Planning Meals:

Batch Cooking: Prepare a larger batch and store it in the refrigerator or freezer for quick meals.
Smooth Texture: Ensure a smooth texture by blending thoroughly, especially for younger babies.
Flavor Variety: Experiment with adding other baby-safe vegetables like peas or sweet potatoes for added nutrition and flavor.

Storage Information:

Refrigerator: Store the prepared puree in an airtight container for up to 3 days.
Freezer: Portion the puree into small, airtight containers or ice cube trays and freeze for up to 1 month. Thaw in the refrigerator overnight before reheating.

Instructions:

1. **Prepare the Ingredients:**
Peel and dice the carrot and potato.
Wash and chop the broccoli into small florets.
Dice the zucchini.
2. **Cook the Rabbit:**
In a small saucepan, add the diced rabbit meat and water or vegetable broth.
Bring to a boil, then reduce the heat to low, cover, and simmer for about 15 minutes, or until the rabbit is cooked through and tender.
3. **Cook the Vegetables:**
Add the diced carrot, potato, broccoli, and zucchini to the saucepan with the rabbit. Continue to simmer for an additional 15 minutes, or until all the vegetables are tender.
4. **Blend the Mixture:**
Remove the saucepan from the heat and let it cool slightly.
Use an immersion blender to puree the mixture until smooth. Alternatively, transfer the cooked rabbit and vegetables along with any remaining liquid to a blender and blend until smooth.
If necessary, add more water or broth to reach the desired consistency.
5. **Serve:**
Allow the puree to cool to a safe temperature before serving.

Nutritional Value per Serving (Approximate):
Calories: 100 Proteins: 9g Fats: 2g Carbohydrates: 12g

TODDLER

BREAKFAST

5 Minutes

10 Minutes

2 servings

Banana Pancakes

Ingredients:

·1 ripe banana
·1 egg
·1/4 cup whole wheat flour
·1/4 cup milk (whole milk or any milk your toddler drinks)
·1/4 teaspoon baking powder
·1/4 teaspoon cinnamon (optional)
·1 teaspoon butter or oil for cooking

Practical Tips for Preparing and Planning Meals:

Batch Cooking: Make a larger batch and store leftovers in the refrigerator or freezer for quick meals.
Easy Eating: Cut the pancakes into small pieces for easy toddler self-feeding.
Flavor Variety: Add other mix-ins like blueberries, grated apples, or finely chopped nuts for added nutrition and flavor.

Storage Information:

Refrigerator: Store the prepared pancakes in an airtight container for up to 3 days.
Freezer: Place the pancakes in one layer on a baking sheet, then move them to a container with a tight lid and put them in the freezer for up to 1 month. Thaw in the refrigerator overnight or reheat from frozen.

Instructions:

1. **Prepare the Batter:**
In a medium bowl, mash the ripe banana with a fork until smooth.
Whisk the egg in thoroughly after adding it.
Add the whole wheat flour, milk, baking powder, and cinnamon (if using). Mix until the batter is smooth.
2. **Cook the Pancakes:**
Heat a non-stick skillet over medium heat and add a little butter or oil.
Pour small amounts of batter onto the skillet to form pancakes (about 2-3 inches in diameter).
Cook for about 2 minutes on each side, or until golden brown and cooked through.
3. **Serve:**
Allow the pancakes to cool slightly before serving to your toddler.

Nutritional Value per Serving (Approximate):
Calories: 110 Proteins: 4g Fats: 2g Carbohydrates: 20g

5 Minutes

0 Minutes

2 servings

Yogurt Parfait

Ingredients:

·1 cup plain whole milk yogurt
·1/2 cup fresh or frozen berries (such as strawberries, blueberries, or raspberries)
·1/4 cup granola (look for low-sugar options suitable for toddlers)
·1 tablespoon honey or maple syrup (optional, for toddlers over 1 year old)

Practical Tips for Preparing and Planning Meals:

Batch Preparation: Prepare individual components ahead of time and assemble the parfaits quickly when needed.
Customization: Customize the parfait with your toddler's favorite fruits or add-ins like chopped nuts or seeds.
Texture Variety: Keep the layers distinct to offer a variety of textures that toddlers can explore.

Storage Information:

Refrigerator: Store the components (yogurt, berries, granola) separately in airtight containers for up to 3 days. Assemble just before serving to maintain the texture.

Instructions:

1. **Prepare the Ingredients:**
Wash the fresh berries if using, or thaw frozen berries.
If desired, lightly mash the berries with a fork for easier eating.
2. **Assemble the Parfait:**
In a small cup or bowl, add a layer of yogurt.
Add a layer of berries on top of the yogurt.
Sprinkle a layer of granola over the berries.
Repeat the layers until you reach the top of the cup or bowl, finishing with a sprinkle of granola on top.
3. **Add Sweetener (Optional):**
Drizzle a small amount of honey or maple syrup over the top if using (only for toddlers over 1 year old).
4. **Serve:**
Serve immediately.

Nutritional Value per Serving (Approximate):
Calories: 120 Proteins: 6g Fats: 3g Carbohydrates: 18g

5 Minutes

5 Minutes

2 servings

Scrambled Eggs with Spinach

Ingredients:

·*2 large eggs*
·*1/4 cup fresh spinach leaves, washed and chopped*
·*1 tablespoon whole milk or water*
·*1 teaspoon butter or olive oil*
·*A pinch of salt (optional)*

Practical Tips for Preparing and Planning Meals:

Batch Cooking: *While scrambled eggs are best fresh, you can whisk the eggs and chop the spinach ahead of time for quicker preparation.*
Texture Variety: *For a softer texture, cook the eggs on low heat, stirring frequently.*
Flavor Variety: *Add a small amount of grated cheese or finely chopped herbs for extra flavor.*

Storage Information:

Refrigerator: *Store any leftovers in an airtight container for up to 1 day. Reheat gently on the stovetop or in the microwave.*

Instructions:

1. **Prepare the Spinach:**
Wash and chop the fresh spinach leaves.
2. **Whisk the Eggs:**
In a small bowl, whisk together the eggs, milk or water, and a pinch of salt (if using).
3. **Cook the Eggs:**
Heat the butter or olive oil in a non-stick skillet over medium heat.
Add the chopped spinach to the skillet and cook for about 1 minute, or until wilted.
Pour the egg mixture into the skillet with the spinach.
Gently stir the eggs with a spatula, pushing them from the edges toward the center until they are softly set and slightly runny in places, about 2-3 minutes.
4. **Serve:**
Remove the skillet from the heat and let the residual heat finish cooking the eggs.
Allow the scrambled eggs to cool to a safe temperature before serving.

Nutritional Value per Serving (Approximate):
Calories: 100 Proteins: 6g Fats: 7g Carbohydrates: 2g

10 Minutes

15 Minutes

2 servings

Whole Wheat Pancakes with Berries

Ingredients:

·1/2 cup whole wheat flour
·1/2 teaspoon baking powder
·1/4 teaspoon baking soda
·1/4 teaspoon cinnamon (optional)
·1/2 cup milk (whole milk or any milk your toddler drinks)
·1 egg
·1 tablespoon unsweetened applesauce or mashed banana (optional for sweetness)
·1 tablespoon butter or oil for cooking
·1/2 cup fresh or frozen berries (such as blueberries, strawberries, or raspberries)

Practical Tips for Preparing and Planning Meals:

Batch Cooking: Make a larger batch and store leftovers in the refrigerator or freezer for quick meals.
Easy Eating: Cut the pancakes into small pieces for easy toddler self-feeding.
Flavor Variety: Add other mix-ins like grated apples, chopped nuts, or a dash of vanilla extract for added nutrition and flavor.

Storage Information:

Refrigerator: Store the prepared pancakes in an airtight container for up to 3 days.
Freezer: Place the pancakes in one layer on a baking sheet, then move them to a container that seals tightly and put them in the freezer for up to 1 month. Thaw in the refrigerator overnight or reheat from frozen.

Instructions:

1. **Prepare the Batter:**
In a medium bowl, whisk together the whole wheat flour, baking powder, baking soda, and cinnamon (if using).
In another bowl, whisk together the milk, egg, and applesauce or mashed banana.
Pour wet ingredients into dry ingredients and stir until just combined. Do not overmix; a few lumps are fine.
2. **Cook the Pancakes:**
Heat a non-stick skillet or griddle over medium heat and add a small amount of butter or oil.
Pour small amounts of batter onto the skillet to form pancakes (about 2-3 inches in diameter).
A few berries should be dropped into each pancake while the batter is still moist.
Cook for about 2 minutes, or until bubbles form on the surface and the edges look set.
Flip and cook for another 1-2 minutes, or until golden brown and cooked through.
3. **Serve:**
Allow the pancakes to cool slightly before serving to your toddler.
Serve with additional fresh berries on top if desired.

Nutritional Value per Serving (Approximate):

Calories: 130 Proteins: 4g Fats: 4g Carbohydrates: 20g

5 Minutes

0 Minutes

2 servings

Cottage Cheese with Pineapple

Ingredients:

·1 cup cottage cheese (full-fat or low-fat)
·1/2 cup fresh pineapple, diced (or canned pineapple chunks in juice, drained)
·1 teaspoon honey or maple syrup (optional, for toddlers over 1 year old)

Practical Tips for Preparing and Planning Meals:

Batch Preparation: Prepare individual portions ahead of time and store them in the refrigerator for quick meals or snacks.
Texture Variety: For a smoother texture, you can blend the cottage cheese and pineapple together.
Flavor Variety: Experiment with adding other fruits like diced peaches, mango, or berries for different flavors.

Storage Information:

Refrigerator: Store the prepared cottage cheese and pineapple in an airtight container for up to 2 days. Stir well before serving.

Instructions:

1. **Prepare the Pineapple:**
If using fresh pineapple, peel, core, and dice it into small chunks. If using canned pineapple, drain the juice and cut the chunks into smaller pieces if needed.
2. **Combine Ingredients:**
In a small bowl, combine the cottage cheese and diced pineapple.
Stir gently to mix.
3. **Add Sweetener (Optional):**
If desired, drizzle a small amount of honey or maple syrup over the mixture (only for toddlers over 1 year old).
4. **Serve:**
Serve immediately or store in the refrigerator until ready to serve.

Nutritional Value per Serving (Approximate):
Calories: 100 Proteins: 8g Fats: 2g Carbohydrates: 12g

10 Minutes

15 Minutes

2 servings

Ricotta Pancakes

Ingredients:

- 1/2 cup ricotta cheese
- 1/2 cup whole wheat flour
- 1/4 cup milk (whole milk or any milk your toddler drinks)
- 1 egg
- 1 tablespoon honey or maple syrup (optional, for toddlers over 1 year old)
- 1/2 teaspoon baking powder
- 1/4 teaspoon vanilla extract (optional)
- 1 teaspoon butter or oil for cooking

Practical Tips for Preparing and Planning Meals:

Batch Cooking: Make a larger batch and store leftovers in the refrigerator or freezer for quick meals.
Easy Eating: Cut the pancakes into small pieces for easy toddler self-feeding.
Flavor Variety: Add other mix-ins like blueberries, grated apples, or finely chopped nuts for added nutrition and flavor.

Storage Information:

Refrigerator: Store the prepared pancakes in an airtight container for up to 3 days.
Freezer: Freeze the pancakes in a single layer on a baking sheet, then transfer to an airtight container and freeze for up to 1 month. Thaw in the refrigerator overnight or reheat from frozen.

Instructions:

1. **Prepare the Batter:**
In a medium bowl, whisk together the ricotta cheese, milk, egg, honey or maple syrup (if using), and vanilla extract (if using). Add the whole wheat flour and baking powder, and stir until just combined. Do not overmix; a few lumps are fine.
2. **Cook the Pancakes:**
Heat a non-stick skillet or griddle over medium heat and add a small amount of butter or oil.
Pour small amounts of batter onto the skillet to form pancakes (about 2-3 inches in diameter).
Cook for about 2-3 minutes, or until bubbles form on the surface and the edges look set. Flip and cook for another 1-2 minutes, or until golden brown and cooked through.
3. **Serve:**
Allow the pancakes to cool slightly before serving to your toddler.

Nutritional Value per Serving (Approximate):
Calories: 140 Proteins: 6g Fats: 5g Carbohydrates: 18g

10 Minutes

30 Minutes

2 servings

Cottage Cheese Casserole

Ingredients:

·1 cup cottage cheese (full-fat or low-fat)
·1/4 cup whole wheat flour
·1/4 cup milk (whole milk or any milk your toddler drinks)
·1 egg
·1 tablespoon honey or maple syrup (optional, for toddlers over 1 year old)
·1/2 teaspoon baking powder
·1/4 teaspoon vanilla extract (optional)
·1/4 cup fresh or frozen berries (such as blueberries or raspberries)
·1 teaspoon butter or oil for greasing

Practical Tips for Preparing and Planning Meals:

Batch Cooking: Make a larger batch and store leftovers in the refrigerator for quick meals.
Texture Variety: For a smoother texture, blend the cottage cheese before mixing it with other ingredients.
Flavor Variety: Add other mix-ins like grated apples, chopped nuts, or cinnamon for added nutrition and flavor.

Storage Information:

Refrigerator: Store the prepared casserole in an airtight container for up to 3 days.
Freezer: Freeze individual portions in airtight containers for up to 1 month. Thaw in the refrigerator overnight before reheating.

Instructions:

1. **Prepare the Batter:**
In a medium bowl, whisk together the cottage cheese, milk, egg, honey or maple syrup (if using), and vanilla extract (if using). Add the whole wheat flour and baking powder, and stir until just combined. Do not overmix.
Gently fold in the berries.
2. **Prepare the Baking Dish:**
Preheat the oven to 350°F (175°C).
Grease a small baking dish with butter or oil.
3. **Bake the Casserole:**
Pour the batter into the prepared baking dish.
Bake for about 25-30 minutes, or until the casserole is set and golden brown on top. Insert a toothpick into the center; if it comes out clean, the casserole is done.
4. **Serve:**
Allow the casserole to cool slightly before serving to your toddler. Cut into small, manageable pieces.

Nutritional Value per Serving (Approximate):
Calories: 150 Proteins: 10g Fats: 6g Carbohydrates: 12g

10 Minutes

20 Minutes

6 servings

Egg and Broccoli Baking Cups

Ingredients:

·3 large eggs
·1/2 cup fresh broccoli florets, finely chopped
·1/4 cup shredded cheese (cheddar, mozzarella, or your toddler's favorite)
·1/4 cup milk (whole milk or any milk your toddler drinks)
·A pinch of salt and pepper (optional)
Non-stick cooking spray or oil for greasing

Practical Tips for Preparing and Planning Meals:

Batch Cooking: Make a larger batch and store leftovers in the refrigerator or freezer for quick meals.
Customization: Add other finely chopped vegetables like bell peppers, spinach, or tomatoes for variety.
Portable Snack: These baking cups are great for on-the-go snacks or meals.

Storage Information:

Refrigerator: Store the prepared baking cups in an airtight container for up to 3 days.
Freezer: Freeze the baking cups in a single layer on a baking sheet, then transfer to an airtight container and freeze for up to 1 month. Thaw in the refrigerator overnight or reheat from frozen.

Instructions:

1. **Prepare the Ingredients:**
Preheat the oven to 350°F (175°C).
Finely chop the broccoli florets.
2. **Whisk the Eggs:**
In a medium bowl, beat the eggs, milk, pepper, and salt (if using).
3. **Assemble the Baking Cups:**
Grease a muffin tin with non-stick cooking spray or oil.
Evenly distribute the chopped broccoli and shredded cheese among the muffin cups.
4. **Pour the Egg Mixture:**
Pour the egg mixture over the broccoli and cheese in each muffin cup, filling them about 3/4 full.
5. **Bake:**
Bake in the preheated oven for about 15-20 minutes, or until the eggs are set and the tops are golden brown.
Insert a toothpick into the center; if it comes out clean, the baking cups are done.
6. **Serve:**
Allow the baking cups to cool slightly before removing them from the muffin tin.
Serve warm or at room temperature.

Nutritional Value per Serving (Approximate):

Calories: 90 Proteins: 6g Fats: 6g Carbohydrates: 2g

10 Minutes

10 Minutes

2 servings

French Toast with Berries

Ingredients:

·2 slices whole wheat bread
·1 large egg
·1/4 cup milk (whole milk or any milk your toddler drinks)
·1/2 teaspoon cinnamon (optional)
·1 teaspoon butter or oil for cooking
·1/2 cup fresh or frozen berries (such as strawberries, blueberries, or raspberries)
·1 teaspoon honey or maple syrup (optional, for toddlers over 1 year old)

Practical Tips for Preparing and Planning Meals:

Batch Cooking: Make a larger batch and store leftovers in the refrigerator for quick meals.
Easy Eating: Cut the French toast into small pieces for easy toddler self-feeding.
Flavor Variety: Experiment with different types of bread or add-ins like vanilla extract or nutmeg for added flavor.

Storage Information:

Refrigerator: Store the prepared French toast in an airtight container for up to 2 days. Reheat gently on the stovetop or in the microwave.
Freezer: Freeze the cooked French toast in a single layer on a baking sheet, then transfer to an airtight container and freeze for up to 1 month. Thaw in the refrigerator overnight or reheat from frozen.

Instructions:

1. **Prepare the Egg Mixture:**
In a shallow bowl, whisk together the egg, milk, and cinnamon (if using).
2. **Dip the Bread:**
Dip each slice of bread into the egg mixture, ensuring both sides are well coated.
3. **Cook the French Toast:**
Heat the butter or oil in a non-stick skillet over medium heat.
Add the coated bread slices and cook for about 2-3 minutes on each side, or until golden brown and cooked through.
4. **Prepare the Berries:**
If using fresh berries, wash them thoroughly. If using frozen berries, thaw them before serving.
5. **Serve:**
Allow the French toast to cool slightly, then cut it into small, manageable pieces for your toddler.
Top with fresh or thawed berries.
Drizzle with a small amount of honey or maple syrup if desired (only for toddlers over 1 year old).

Nutritional Value per Serving (Approximate):

Calories: 160 Proteins: 6g Fats: 5g Carbohydrates: 24g

10 Minutes

10 Minutes

2 servings

Zucchini Waffles with Yogurt

Ingredients:

·1 small zucchini, grated
·1/2 cup whole wheat flour
·1/4 cup milk (whole milk or any milk your toddler drinks)
·1 large egg
·1/4 cup plain whole milk yogurt
·1 tablespoon olive oil or melted butter
·1/2 teaspoon baking powder
·1/4 teaspoon cinnamon (optional)
·Non-stick cooking spray or additional oil for greasing the waffle iron
For Serving:
·1/2 cup plain whole milk yogurt
·Fresh or thawed berries (optional)
·A drizzle of honey or maple syrup (optional, for toddlers over 1 year old)

Practical Tips for Preparing and Planning Meals:

Batch Cooking: Make a larger batch and store leftovers in the refrigerator or freezer for quick meals.
Easy Eating: Cut the waffles into small pieces for easy toddler self-feeding.
Flavor Variety: Experiment with adding other mix-ins like grated carrots, apples, or finely chopped nuts for added nutrition and flavor.

Storage Information:

Refrigerator: Store the prepared waffles in an airtight container for up to 3 days. Reheat gently in the toaster or microwave.
Freezer: Freeze the cooked waffles in a single layer on a baking sheet, then transfer to an airtight container and freeze for up to 1 month. Thaw in the refrigerator overnight or reheat from frozen.

Instructions:

1. **Prepare the Zucchini:**
Grate the zucchini and squeeze out excess moisture using a clean kitchen towel or paper towel.
2. **Prepare the Batter:**
In a medium bowl, whisk together the egg, milk, yogurt, and olive oil or melted butter. In another bowl, combine the whole wheat flour, baking powder, and cinnamon (if using).
Add the dry ingredients to the wet ingredients and stir until just combined. Fold in the grated zucchini.
3. **Cook the Waffles:**
Preheat the waffle iron and grease it with non-stick cooking spray or a little oil.
Pour the batter into the preheated waffle iron and cook according to the manufacturer's instructions, usually about 3-5 minutes, until the waffles are golden brown and cooked through.
4. **Serve:**
Allow the waffles to cool slightly, then cut them into small, manageable pieces for your toddler.
Serve with a dollop of plain yogurt and fresh or thawed berries on top.
Drizzle with a small amount of honey or maple syrup if desired (only for toddlers over 1 year old).

Nutritional Value per Serving (Approximate):

Calories: 140 Proteins: 5g Fats: 6g Carbohydrates: 18g

10 Minutes

30 Minutes

2 servings

Baked Oatmeal with Apple

Ingredients:

·1 cup rolled oats
·1/2 cup milk (whole milk or any milk your toddler drinks)
·1 small apple, peeled, cored, and diced
·1/4 cup unsweetened applesauce
·1 large egg
·1 tablespoon honey or maple syrup (optional, for toddlers over 1 year old)
·1/2 teaspoon baking powder
·1/2 teaspoon cinnamon
·1/4 teaspoon vanilla extract (optional)
·1 tablespoon butter or oil for greasing

Practical Tips for Preparing and Planning Meals:

Batch Cooking: Make a larger batch and store leftovers in the refrigerator for quick meals.
Customization: Add other fruits like blueberries, raisins, or chopped nuts for variety.
Portable Snack: This baked oatmeal is great for on-the-go snacks or meals.

Storage Information:

Refrigerator: Store the prepared baked oatmeal in an airtight container for up to 3 days. Reheat gently in the microwave or enjoy cold.
Freezer: Freeze individual portions in airtight containers for up to 1 month. Thaw in the refrigerator overnight before reheating.

Instructions:

1. **Prepare the Baking Dish:**
Preheat the oven to 350°F (175°C). Grease a small baking dish with butter or oil.
2. **Prepare the Apple:**
Peel, core, and dice the apple into small pieces.
3. **Mix the Wet Ingredients:**
In a medium bowl, mix the milk, applesauce, egg, honey, vanilla extract (if using), and maple syrup (if using) with a mixer.
4. **Combine Dry Ingredients:**
In another bowl, mix the rolled oats, baking powder, and cinnamon.
5. **Assemble the Oatmeal:**
Add the wet ingredients to the dry ingredients and stir until well combined. Fold in the diced apple.
6. **Bake:**
Pour the mixture into the greased baking dish.
Bake for about 30 minutes, or until the top is golden brown and the oatmeal is set. Insert a toothpick into the center; if it comes out clean, the oatmeal is done.
7. **Serve:**
Allow the baked oatmeal to cool slightly before cutting it into small, manageable pieces for your toddler.

Nutritional Value per Serving (Approximate):
Calories: 150 Proteins: 4g Fats: 5g Carbohydrates: 24g

5 Minutes

10 Minutes

2 servings

Egg Burrito

Ingredients:

·2 large eggs
·1/4 cup milk (whole milk or any milk your toddler drinks)
·1/4 cup shredded cheese (cheddar, mozzarella, or your toddler's favorite)
·1/4 cup finely chopped vegetables (such as bell peppers, spinach, or tomatoes)
·2 small whole wheat tortillas
·1 tablespoon butter or olive oil
·A pinch of salt (optional)

Practical Tips for Preparing and Planning Meals:

Batch Cooking: Prepare a larger batch of the egg mixture and store it in the refrigerator for quick meal assembly.
Customization: Add other fillings like cooked beans, avocado, or cooked sausage for variety.
Portable Meal: These burritos are great for on-the-go meals or snacks.

Storage Information:

Refrigerator: Store the prepared burritos in an airtight container for up to 2 days. Reheat gently in the microwave or on the stovetop.
Freezer: Wrap the burritos individually in foil or plastic wrap and freeze for up to 1 month. Thaw in the refrigerator overnight before reheating.

Instructions:

1. **Prepare the Eggs:**
In a small bowl, whisk together the eggs, milk, and a pinch of salt (if using).
2. **Cook the Eggs:**
Heat the butter or olive oil in a non-stick skillet over medium heat.
Add the finely chopped vegetables to the skillet and cook for about 2 minutes, or until softened.
Pour the egg mixture into the skillet with the vegetables.
Stir the eggs with a spatula, moving them from the sides toward the center, until softly set and somewhat runny in parts, about 3-4 minutes.
Sprinkle the shredded cheese over the eggs and cook until the eggs are fully set and the cheese is melted.
3. **Assemble the Burritos:**
Warm the whole wheat tortillas in the microwave for about 20 seconds or in a dry skillet for about 1 minute on each side.
Place half of the scrambled egg mixture in the center of each tortilla.
Fold the sides of the tortilla over the filling, then roll it up from the bottom to form a burrito.
4. **Serve:**
Allow the burritos to cool slightly before serving to your toddler. Cut them into smaller pieces if needed.

Nutritional Value per Serving (Approximate):
Calories: 180 Proteins: 10g Fats: 10g Carbohydrates: 12g

LUNCH

10 Minutes

20 Minutes

2 servings

Veggie Mac and Cheese

Ingredients:

- 1 cup elbow macaroni or small pasta shapes
- 1 cup mixed vegetables (such as broccoli florets, peas, and diced carrots)
- 1 tablespoon butter
- 1 tablespoon all-purpose flour
- 1 cup milk (whole milk or any milk your toddler drinks)
- 1 cup shredded cheese (cheddar, mozzarella, or a blend)
- A pinch of salt (optional)
- A pinch of pepper (optional)

Practical Tips for Preparing and Planning Meals:

Batch Cooking: Prepare a larger batch and store leftovers in the refrigerator for quick meals.
Customization: Use different types of vegetables like spinach, zucchini, or bell peppers for variety.
Texture Variety: For a smoother texture, blend the vegetables before mixing with the pasta and cheese sauce.

Storage Information:

Refrigerator: Store the prepared mac and cheese in an airtight container for up to 3 days. Reheat gently on the stovetop or in the microwave, adding a splash of milk if needed to adjust the consistency.
Freezer: Portion the mac and cheese into small, airtight containers and freeze for up to 1 month. Thaw in the refrigerator overnight before reheating.

Instructions:

1. **Cook the Pasta and Vegetables:**
Bring a large pot of water to a boil. Add the pasta and cook according to package instructions.
In the last 3 minutes of cooking, add the mixed vegetables to the boiling pasta.
After draining, set aside the pasta and veggies.

2. **Prepare the Cheese Sauce:**
In the same pot, melt the butter over medium heat.
Stir in the flour and cook for about 1 minute, until it forms a paste.
Slowly whisk in the milk, continuing to whisk until the mixture is smooth and starts to thicken, about 3-5 minutes.
Take the pot off the heat and mix in the grated cheese until it melts and becomes smooth.
Add a pinch of salt and pepper if desired.

3. **Combine and Serve:**
Add the cooked pasta and vegetables back into the pot with the cheese sauce.
Stir until everything is well coated with the cheese sauce.
Serve immediately. Allow the mac and cheese to cool to a safe temperature before serving to your toddler.

Nutritional Value per Serving (Approximate):

Calories: 250 Proteins: 10g Fats: 10g Carbohydrates: 30g

10 Minutes

0 Minutes

2 servings

Turkey and Avocado Wrap

Ingredients:

·2 small whole wheat tortillas
·4 slices of deli turkey breast (low sodium)
·1 ripe avocado
·1/2 cup shredded lettuce or spinach
·1/4 cup grated carrots
·1/4 cup sliced cucumber
·1 tablespoon cream cheese or hummus (optional)
·A squeeze of lemon or lime juice (optional)

Practical Tips for Preparing and Planning Meals:

Batch Preparation: Prepare the wraps ahead of time and store them in the refrigerator for quick meals or snacks.
Customization: Add other fillings like sliced tomatoes, bell peppers, or cheese for variety.
Portable Meal: These wraps are great for on-the-go meals or lunchboxes.

Storage Information:

Refrigerator: Store the prepared wraps in an airtight container for up to 1 day to maintain freshness.

Instructions:

1. **Prepare the Avocado:**
Cut the avocado in half, remove the pit, and scoop out the flesh into a small bowl.
Mash the avocado with a fork until smooth.
Add a squeeze of lemon or lime juice if desired to prevent browning and add flavor.
2. **Assemble the Wraps:**
Lay the tortillas flat on a clean surface.
Spread a thin layer of cream cheese or hummus on each tortilla (if using).
Spread the mashed avocado evenly over the tortillas.
Layer the turkey slices on top of the avocado.
Add shredded lettuce or spinach, grated carrots, and sliced cucumber.
3. **Roll the Wraps:**
Roll up the tortillas tightly, folding in the sides as you go to create a secure wrap.
Cut each wrap into small, manageable pieces for your toddler.
4. **Serve:**
Serve the wraps immediately or store them in the refrigerator until ready to eat.

Nutritional Value per Serving (Approximate):
Calories: 200 Proteins: 10g Fats: 12g Carbohydrates: 15g

10 Minutes

20 Minutes

2 servings

Grilled Cheese and Tomato Soup

Ingredients:

For the Tomato Soup:
·1 tablespoon olive oil
·1/2 small onion, finely chopped
·1 clove garlic, minced
·1 can (14.5 ounces) diced tomatoes (no salt added)
·1 cup low-sodium vegetable broth
·1/2 cup milk (whole milk or any milk your toddler drinks)
·A pinch of salt and pepper (optional)
·1/4 teaspoon dried basil or thyme (optional)

For the Grilled Cheese:
·4 slices whole wheat bread
·1/2 cup shredded cheese (cheddar, mozzarella, or a blend)
·1 tablespoon butter

Practical Tips for Preparing and Planning Meals:

Batch Cooking: Prepare a larger batch of tomato soup and store leftovers in the refrigerator or freezer for quick meals.
Customization: Add finely chopped vegetables like spinach or bell peppers to the grilled cheese for extra nutrition.
Texture Variety: For a smoother soup, strain the pureed mixture through a fine mesh sieve before adding the milk.

Storage Information:

Refrigerator: Store the prepared tomato soup in an airtight container for up to 3 days. Store the grilled cheese sandwiches in an airtight container for up to 1 day. Reheat gently on the stovetop or in the microwave.
Freezer: Portion the tomato soup into small, airtight containers and freeze for up to 1 month. Thaw in the refrigerator overnight before reheating.

Instructions:

For the Tomato Soup:
1. Sauté the Aromatics:
In a medium saucepan, heat the olive oil over medium heat.
Add the chopped onion and garlic. Sauté for about 5 minutes, or until the onion is soft and translucent.
2. **Cook the Tomatoes:**
Add the diced tomatoes (with their juice) and vegetable broth to the saucepan.
Bring to a boil, then reduce the heat to low and simmer for about 10 minutes.
3. **Blend the Soup:**
Use an immersion blender to puree the soup until smooth. Alternatively, carefully transfer the soup to a blender and blend until smooth.
Return the soup to the saucepan if using a blender.
4. **Add Milk and Seasonings:**
Add salt, pepper, and dried thyme or basil, if using, and stir in the milk.
Heat the soup gently until warmed through, but do not boil.

For the Grilled Cheese:
1. Assemble the Sandwiches:
Place two slices of bread on a clean surface.
Evenly distribute the shredded cheese over the bread slices.
Top with the remaining two slices of bread to form sandwiches.
2. **Grill the Sandwiches:**
Heat a non-stick skillet over medium heat and add half the butter.
Place the sandwiches in the skillet and cook for about 2-3 minutes on each side, or until the bread is golden brown and the cheese is melted.
Add the remaining butter to the skillet as needed.
3. **Serve:**
Allow the grilled cheese sandwiches to cool slightly, then cut them into small, manageable pieces for your toddler.
Serve the grilled cheese alongside a small bowl of warm tomato soup.

Nutritional Value per Serving (Approximate):

Calories: 250 Proteins: 10g Fats: 12g Carbohydrates: 28g

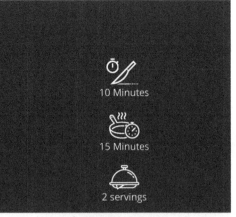

10 Minutes

15 Minutes

2 servings

Chicken and Avocado Salad for Toddlers

Ingredients:

·*1 small boneless, skinless chicken breast (about 4 ounces)*
·*1 ripe avocado*
·*1/2 cup cherry tomatoes, halved*
·*1/4 cup finely chopped cucumber*
·*1 tablespoon olive oil*
·*1 teaspoon lemon juice*
·*A pinch of salt and pepper (optional)*

Practical Tips for Preparing and Planning Meals:

Batch Cooking: *Cook extra chicken breasts and store them in the refrigerator for quick meal assembly.*
Customization: *Add other toddler-friendly vegetables like finely chopped bell peppers, grated carrots, or sweet corn for variety.*
Flavor Variety: *Experiment with different dressings or add-ins like a sprinkle of mild cheese or a few croutons for added texture.*

Storage Information:

Refrigerator: *Store any leftovers in an airtight container for up to 1 day. Note that avocado may brown slightly but is still safe to eat.*

Instructions:

1. **Cook the Chicken (if not using pre-cooked):**
Bring a small pot of water to a boil. Add the chicken breast and reduce to a simmer. Cook for about 12-15 minutes, or until the chicken is fully cooked and no longer pink inside.
Remove the chicken from the water and let it cool slightly. Once cooled, chop the chicken into small, bite-sized pieces.
2. **Prepare the Avocado:**
Cut the avocado in half, remove the pit, and scoop out the flesh into a small bowl. Dice the avocado into small pieces.
3. **Assemble the Salad:**
In a medium bowl, combine the cooked chicken, diced avocado, cherry tomatoes, and cucumber.
Drizzle the olive oil and lemon juice over the salad.
Gently toss to combine all ingredients. Season with a pinch of salt and pepper if desired.
4. **Serve:**
Serve the chicken and avocado salad immediately.

Nutritional Value per Serving (Approximate):
Calories: 180 Proteins: 12g Fats: 12g Carbohydrates: 6g

10 Minutes

0 Minutes

2 servings

Tomato and Mozzarella Salad for Toddlers

Ingredients:

- 1 cup cherry tomatoes, halved
- 1/2 cup fresh mozzarella balls (bocconcini or ciliegine), halved
- 1 tablespoon olive oil
- 1 teaspoon balsamic vinegar (optional)
- A few fresh basil leaves, chopped or torn (optional)
- A pinch of salt and pepper (optional)

Practical Tips for Preparing and Planning Meals:

Batch Preparation: Prepare the salad ingredients ahead of time and store them separately in the refrigerator. Assemble just before serving.
Customization: Add other toddler-friendly ingredients like diced cucumber, sliced bell peppers, or sweet corn for extra flavor and nutrition.
Flavor Variety: Experiment with different herbs such as oregano or parsley for a different taste.

Storage Information:

Refrigerator: Store any leftovers in an airtight container for up to 1 day.

Instructions:

1. **Prepare the Ingredients:**
Wash and halve the cherry tomatoes.
Drain the mozzarella balls and halve them if they are not already halved.
Wash and chop or tear the fresh basil leaves if using.
2. **Assemble the Salad:**
In a medium bowl, combine the halved cherry tomatoes and mozzarella balls.
Drizzle the olive oil over the top and add the balsamic vinegar if using.
Gently toss to combine all ingredients.
Add the chopped or torn basil leaves and season with a pinch of salt and pepper if desired.
3. **Serve:**
Serve the tomato and mozzarella salad immediately.

Nutritional Value per Serving (Approximate):
Calories: 150 Proteins: 8g Fats: 10g Carbohydrates: 6g

Hummus and Crudités for Toddlers

Ingredients:

For the Hummus:
·Half a cup of rinsed and drained canned chickpeas
·1 tablespoon tahini
·1 tablespoon olive oil
·1 tablespoon lemon juice
·1 small clove garlic, minced (optional)
·1-2 tablespoons water (as needed)
·A pinch of salt (optional)
For the Crudités:
·1 small carrot, peeled and cut into sticks
·1/2 cucumber, sliced into sticks
·1 small bell pepper, sliced into sticks
·1 small handful of cherry tomatoes, halved

Practical Tips for Preparing and Planning Meals:

Batch Preparation: Prepare a larger batch of hummus and store it in the refrigerator for up to 5 days. Cut vegetables ahead of time and store them in an airtight container in the refrigerator.
Customization: Add other toddler-friendly vegetables like snap peas, celery sticks, or broccoli florets for variety.
Flavor Variety: Experiment with different hummus flavors by adding roasted red peppers, avocado, or a sprinkle of paprika.

Storage Information:

Refrigerator: Store the prepared hummus in an airtight container for up to 5 days. Store cut vegetables in an airtight container for up to 2 days.

Instructions:

Prepare the Hummus:
1. **Blend the Ingredients:**
In a food processor or blender, combine the chickpeas, tahini, olive oil, lemon juice, and minced garlic (if using).
Blend until smooth, adding water a tablespoon at a time until the hummus reaches the desired consistency.
2. **Season:**
Add a pinch of salt if desired and blend again to incorporate.
Prepare the Crudités:
1.**Cut the Vegetables:**
Peel and cut the carrot into sticks.
Slice the cucumber into sticks.
Slice the bell pepper into sticks.
Halve the cherry tomatoes.
Assemble and Serve:
1. **Plate the Hummus and Crudités:**
Spoon the hummus into a small bowl. Arrange the vegetable sticks and cherry tomatoes around the hummus.
2. **Serve:**
Serve the hummus and crudités immediately.

Nutritional Value per Serving (Approximate):

Calories: 100 Proteins: 3g Fats: 5g Carbohydrates: 12g

10 Minutes

20 Minutes

2 servings

Pasta with Veggie Sauce for Toddlers

Ingredients:

·One cup of tiny pasta forms, such macaroni or tiny shells
·1 tablespoon olive oil
·1/2 small onion, finely chopped
·1 clove garlic, minced
·1 small carrot, peeled and diced
·1 small zucchini, diced
·1/2 cup broccoli florets, chopped
·1 can (14.5 ounces) diced tomatoes (no salt added)
·1/4 cup grated Parmesan cheese (optional)
·A pinch of salt and pepper (optional)
·Fresh basil or parsley for garnish (optional)

Practical Tips for Preparing and Planning Meals:

Batch Cooking: Prepare a larger batch of veggie sauce and store leftovers in the refrigerator or freezer for quick meals.
Customization: Use any combination of toddler-friendly vegetables that your child enjoys.
Texture Variety: For a chunkier sauce, finely chop the vegetables instead of blending them.

Storage Information:

Refrigerator: Store the prepared pasta and veggie sauce in an airtight container for up to 3 days. Reheat gently on the stovetop or in the microwave.
Freezer: Portion the veggie sauce into small, airtight containers and freeze for up to 1 month. Thaw in the refrigerator overnight before reheating.

Instructions:

1. **Cook the Pasta:**
Bring a large pot of water to a boil. Add the pasta and cook according to the package instructions. Drain and set aside.
2. **Prepare the Veggie Sauce:**
In a large skillet, heat the olive oil over medium heat.
Add the chopped onion and garlic. Sauté for about 3-5 minutes, or until the onion is soft and translucent.
Add the diced carrot, zucchini, and chopped broccoli. Cook for about 5-7 minutes, or until the vegetables are tender.
Add the diced tomatoes (with their juice) to the skillet. Stir to combine and bring to a simmer. Cook for an additional 5-7 minutes, or until the sauce has thickened slightly.
3. **Blend the Sauce (Optional):**
For a smoother sauce, use an immersion blender to puree the sauce until it reaches the desired consistency. Alternatively, carefully transfer the sauce to a blender and blend until smooth, then return it to the skillet.
4. **Combine and Serve:**
Add the cooked pasta to the skillet with the veggie sauce. Stir to coat the pasta evenly with the sauce.
Season with a pinch of salt and pepper if desired.
Serve the pasta topped with grated Parmesan cheese and a sprinkle of fresh basil or parsley if desired.

Nutritional Value per Serving (Approximate):

Calories: 200 Proteins: 6g Fats: 5g Carbohydrates: 32

10 Minutes

15 Minutes

2 servings

Broccoli Pesto Pasta for Toddlers

Ingredients:

·One cup of tiny pasta forms, such macaroni or tiny shells
·1 cup broccoli florets, chopped
·1/4 cup fresh basil leaves
·1/4 cup grated Parmesan cheese
·1/4 cup olive oil
·1 small clove garlic (optional)
·1 tablespoon lemon juice
·2 tablespoons pine nuts or walnuts (optional)
·A pinch of salt and pepper (optional)

Practical Tips for Preparing and Planning Meals:

Batch Cooking: Prepare a larger batch of pesto and store leftovers in the refrigerator or freezer for quick meals.
Customization: Use any combination of toddler-friendly vegetables that your child enjoys.
Texture Variety: For a chunkier pesto, pulse the ingredients in the food processor instead of blending until smooth.

Storage Information:

Refrigerator: Store the prepared pasta and pesto in an airtight container for up to 3 days. Reheat gently on the stovetop or in the microwave.
Freezer: Portion the pesto into small, airtight containers and freeze for up to 1 month. Thaw in the refrigerator overnight before using.

Instructions:

1. **Cook the Pasta and Broccoli:**
Bring a large pot of water to a boil. Add the pasta and cook according to the package instructions.
During the last 3 minutes of the pasta cooking time, add the broccoli florets to the boiling water with the pasta.
Drain the pasta and broccoli and set aside.

2. **Prepare the Pesto:**
In a food processor or blender, combine the fresh basil leaves, grated Parmesan cheese, olive oil, garlic (if using), lemon juice, and pine nuts or walnuts (if using).
Blend until smooth, adding a little water if necessary to achieve the desired consistency.
Season with a pinch of salt and pepper if desired.

3. **Combine and Serve:**
In a large bowl, toss the cooked pasta and broccoli with the prepared pesto until evenly coated.
Serve the pasta immediately, topped with extra grated Parmesan cheese if desired.

Nutritional Value per Serving (Approximate):

Calories: 220 Proteins: 8g Fats: 9g Carbohydrates: 28g

15 Minutes

20 Minutes

2 servings

Baked Quinoa Chicken Nuggets

Ingredients:

·1/2 cup quinoa, rinsed
·1 cup water
·1 small boneless, skinless chicken breast (about 4 ounces), cut into bite-sized pieces
·1/4 cup whole wheat flour
·1 large egg, beaten
·1/2 cup breadcrumbs (whole wheat or panko)
·1/4 teaspoon garlic powder (optional)
·1/4 teaspoon onion powder (optional)
·A pinch of salt and pepper (optional)
·Olive oil or cooking spray for greasing

Practical Tips for Preparing and Planning Meals:

Batch Cooking: Make a larger batch and store leftovers in the refrigerator or freezer for quick meals.
Customization: Add finely grated Parmesan cheese or dried herbs to the quinoa mixture for extra flavor.
Portable Snack: These nuggets are great for on-the-go meals or lunchboxes.

Storage Information:

Refrigerator: Store the prepared nuggets in an airtight container for up to 3 days. Reheat gently in the oven or microwave.
Freezer: Freeze the cooked nuggets in a single layer on a baking sheet, then transfer to an airtight container and freeze for up to 1 month. Reheat from frozen in the oven at 375°F (190°C) until heated through.

Instructions:

1. **Cook the Quinoa:**
In a small saucepan, combine the rinsed quinoa and water.
Bring to a boil, then reduce the heat to low, cover, and simmer for about 15 minutes, or until the quinoa is cooked and the water is absorbed.
Fluff the quinoa with a fork and let it cool slightly.
2. **Prepare the Chicken Nuggets:**
Preheat the oven to 400°F (200°C).
Grease a baking sheet with olive oil or cooking spray.
Set up a breading station with three shallow bowls: one with whole wheat flour, one with the beaten egg, and one with the cooked quinoa mixed with breadcrumbs, garlic powder, onion powder, salt, and pepper (if using).
3. **Bread the Chicken:**
Coat each chicken piece in the flour, then dip it in the beaten egg, and finally coat it with the quinoa and breadcrumb mixture. Press the quinoa mixture onto the chicken to ensure it sticks.
4. **Bake the Nuggets:**
Place the breaded chicken pieces on the greased baking sheet.
Lightly spray or drizzle the nuggets with a little olive oil.
Bake for about 15-20 minutes, or until the chicken is cooked through and the nuggets are golden brown. Turn the nuggets halfway through cooking for even browning.
5. **Serve:**
Allow the nuggets to cool slightly before serving to your toddler. Serve with a dipping sauce like yogurt or ketchup if desired.

Nutritional Value per Serving (Approximate):

Calories: 200 Proteins: 15g Fats: 7g Carbohydrates: 18g

10 Minutes

10 Minutes

2 servings

Creamy Pasta Salad

Ingredients:

·**One cup of tiny pasta forms, such macaroni or tiny shells**
·**1/4 cup plain Greek yogurt**
·**1 tablespoon mayonnaise (optional for extra creaminess)**
·**1/2 cup diced cooked chicken or turkey (optional)**
·**1/4 cup finely chopped cucumber**
·**1/4 cup finely chopped bell pepper**
·**1/4 cup halved cherry tomatoes**
·**1/4 cup grated carrot**
·**1 tablespoon lemon juice**
·**1 teaspoon honey or maple syrup (optional)**
·**A pinch of salt and pepper (optional)**
·**Fresh herbs like parsley or dill for garnish (optional)**

Practical Tips for Preparing and Planning Meals:

Batch Cooking: Prepare a larger batch and store leftovers in the refrigerator for quick meals or snacks.
Customization: Add other toddler-friendly vegetables like peas, corn, or finely chopped spinach for extra nutrition.
Texture Variety: For a smoother texture, finely chop all the vegetables.

Storage Information:

Refrigerator: Store the prepared pasta salad in an airtight container for up to 3 days. Stir well before serving.

Instructions:

1. **Cook the Pasta:**
Bring a large pot of water to a boil. Add the pasta and cook according to package instructions.
Drain the pasta and rinse it under cold water to cool it down. Set aside.
2. **Prepare the Dressing:**
In a small bowl, whisk together the Greek yogurt, mayonnaise (if using), lemon juice, and honey or maple syrup (if using).
Add a pinch of salt and pepper if desired.
3. **Combine the Ingredients:**
In a large bowl, combine the cooked pasta, diced chicken or turkey (if using), chopped cucumber, bell pepper, cherry tomatoes, and grated carrot.
Pour the dressing over the pasta mixture and toss until everything is well coated.
4. **Serve:**
Garnish with fresh herbs like parsley or dill if desired.
Serve immediately or chill in the refrigerator for a refreshing cold salad.

Nutritional Value per Serving (Approximate):
Calories: 180 Proteins: 6g Fats: 7g Carbohydrates: 24g

15 Minutes

15 Minutes

2 servings

Chicken Skewers with Vegetables

Ingredients:

·1 small boneless, skinless chicken breast (about 4 ounces), cut into bite-sized pieces
·1 small bell pepper, diced
·1 small zucchini, sliced into rounds
·1/2 small red onion, cut into chunks
·1/2 cup cherry tomatoes
·1 tablespoon olive oil
·1 teaspoon lemon juice
·1/2 teaspoon dried oregano
·1/2 teaspoon garlic powder
·A pinch of salt and pepper (optional)
·Wooden skewers (soaked in water for 30 minutes if using a grill)

Practical Tips for Preparing and Planning Meals:

Batch Cooking: Prepare extra skewers and store leftovers in the refrigerator for quick meals.
Customization: Use any combination of toddler-friendly vegetables that your child enjoys.
Portable Meal: These skewers are great for on-the-go meals or picnics.

Storage Information:

Refrigerator: Store the cooked skewers in an airtight container for up to 3 days. Reheat gently on the stovetop, in the oven, or in the microwave.

Instructions:

1. **Prepare the Marinade:**
In a small bowl, whisk together the olive oil, lemon juice, dried oregano, garlic powder, salt, and pepper (if using).
2. **Marinate the Chicken and Vegetables:**
In a large bowl, combine the chicken pieces and vegetables.
Pour the marinade over the chicken and vegetables, tossing to coat evenly.
Let marinate for at least 10 minutes (or up to 30 minutes for more flavor).
3. **Assemble the Skewers:**
Thread the marinated chicken pieces and vegetables onto the wooden skewers, alternating between chicken and vegetables.
4. **Cook the Skewers:**
Grill Method: Preheat the grill to medium-high heat. Grill the skewers for about 5-7 minutes on each side, or until the chicken is cooked through and the vegetables are tender.
Oven Method: Preheat the oven to 400°F (200°C). Place the skewers on a baking sheet lined with parchment paper. Bake for about 15 minutes, turning halfway through, until the chicken is cooked through and the vegetables are tender.
5. **Serve:**
Allow the skewers to cool slightly before serving to your toddler. Remove the chicken and vegetables from the skewers and cut into small, manageable pieces if needed.

Nutritional Value per Serving (Approximate):
Calories: 200 Proteins: 20g Fats: 7g Carbohydrates: 12g

15 Minutes

20 Minutes

2 servings

Turkey Meatballs with Cream Sauce

Ingredients:

For the Meatballs:
- 1/2 pound ground turkey
- 1/4 cup breadcrumbs (whole wheat or panko)
- 1 egg
- 1/4 cup grated Parmesan cheese
- 1 small carrot, grated
- 1 small zucchini, grated
- 1 clove garlic, minced
- 1/2 teaspoon dried oregano
- A pinch of salt and pepper (optional)
- 1 tablespoon olive oil (for cooking)

For the Cream Sauce:
- 1 tablespoon butter
- 1 tablespoon all-purpose flour
- 1 cup milk (whole milk or any milk your toddler drinks)
- 1/4 cup grated Parmesan cheese
- A pinch of salt and pepper (optional)

Practical Tips for Preparing and Planning Meals:

Batch Cooking: Make a larger batch of meatballs and store leftovers in the refrigerator or freezer for quick meals.
Customization: Add finely chopped herbs like parsley or basil to the meatball mixture for extra flavor.
Portable Meal: These meatballs are great for on-the-go meals or lunchboxes.

Storage Information:

Refrigerator: Store the cooked meatballs and sauce in an airtight container for up to 3 days. Reheat gently on the stovetop or in the microwave.
Freezer: Freeze the cooked meatballs without the sauce in a single layer on a baking sheet, then transfer to an airtight container and freeze for up to 1 month. Thaw in the refrigerator overnight before reheating and adding the sauce.

Instructions:

Prepare the Meatballs:
1. **Mix the Ingredients:**
In a large bowl, combine the ground turkey, breadcrumbs, egg, grated Parmesan cheese, grated carrot, grated zucchini, minced garlic, dried oregano, salt, and pepper (if using).
Mix well until all ingredients are evenly combined.
2. **Form the Meatballs:**
Shape the mixture into small meatballs, about 1-inch in diameter.
3. **Cook the Meatballs:**
Heat the olive oil in a large skillet over medium heat. Add the meatballs to the skillet and cook for about 8-10 minutes, turning occasionally, until the meatballs are browned on all sides and cooked through.
Remove the meatballs from the skillet and set aside.

Prepare the Cream Sauce:
1. **Make the Roux:**
In the same skillet, melt the butter over medium heat.
Stir in the flour and cook for about 1 minute, until it forms a paste.
2. **Add the Milk:**
Gradually whisk in the milk, continuing to whisk until the mixture is smooth and begins to thicken, about 3-5 minutes.
3. **Finish the Sauce:**
Stir in the grated Parmesan cheese and continue to cook until the cheese is melted and the sauce is creamy.
Add a pinch of salt and pepper if desired.

Combine and Serve:
1. **Combine the Meatballs and Sauce:**
Return the cooked meatballs to the skillet with the cream sauce.
Stir gently to coat the meatballs with the sauce and heat through.
2. **Serve:**
Allow the meatballs and sauce to cool slightly before serving to your toddler.
Serve with a side of steamed vegetables, mashed potatoes, or pasta if desired.

Nutritional Value per Serving (Approximate):

Calories: 220 Proteins: 15g Fats: 12g Carbohydrates: 10g

DINNER

15 Minutes

30 Minutes

2 servings

Chicken and Sweet Potato Casserole

Ingredients:

·*1 small boneless, skinless chicken breast (about 4 ounces), diced*
·*1 medium sweet potato, peeled and diced*
·*1/2 small onion, finely chopped*
·*1 small carrot, peeled and diced*
·*1/2 cup broccoli florets, chopped*
·*1/2 cup shredded cheese (cheddar or mozzarella)*
·*1/2 cup milk (whole milk or any milk your toddler drinks)*
·*1 tablespoon olive oil*
·*1 tablespoon all-purpose flour*
·*1/2 teaspoon dried thyme (optional)*
·*A pinch of salt and pepper (optional)*

Practical Tips for Preparing and Planning Meals:

Batch Cooking: *Prepare a larger batch and store leftovers in the refrigerator for quick meals.*
Customization: *Add other toddler-friendly vegetables like peas or corn for extra nutrition.*
Texture Variety: *For a smoother texture, mash the sweet potato slightly before combining with the other ingredients.*

Storage Information:

Refrigerator: *Store the prepared casserole in an airtight container for up to 3 days. Reheat gently in the oven or microwave.*
Freezer: *Portion the casserole into small, airtight containers and freeze for up to 1 month. Thaw in the refrigerator overnight before reheating.*

Instructions:

1.   **Prepare the Ingredients:**
Preheat the oven to 375°F (190°C).
Peel and dice the sweet potato and carrot.
Chop the onion and broccoli.
Dice the chicken breast.
2.   **Cook the Chicken and Vegetables:**
In a large skillet, heat the olive oil over medium heat.
Add the diced chicken and cook until browned and cooked through, about 5-7 minutes. Remove the chicken from the skillet and set aside.
In the same skillet, add the chopped onion, diced sweet potato, carrot, and broccoli. Cook for about 5 minutes, until the vegetables are slightly softened.
3.   **Make the Sauce:**
Sprinkle the flour over the vegetables in the skillet and stir to combine.
Gradually add the milk, stirring constantly until the mixture thickens, about 2-3 minutes.
Add the dried thyme, salt, and pepper if desired.
4.   **Combine and Bake:**
In a baking dish, combine the cooked chicken, vegetable mixture, and shredded cheese. Stir to combine.
Bake in the preheated oven for about 20 minutes, until the casserole is bubbly and the top is golden brown.
5.   **Serve:**
Allow the casserole to cool slightly before serving to your toddler.

Nutritional Value per Serving (Approximate):

Calories: 250 Proteins: 15g Fats: 8g Carbohydrates: 28g

10 Minutes

20 Minutes

2 servings

Baked Salmon with Green Beans

Ingredients:

- *1 small salmon fillet (about 4 ounces)*
- *1 cup green beans, trimmed and cut into bite-sized pieces*
- *1 tablespoon olive oil*
- *1 teaspoon lemon juice*
- *1/2 teaspoon dried dill (optional)*
- *A pinch of salt and pepper (optional)*
- *1 clove garlic, minced (optional)*

Practical Tips for Preparing and Planning Meals:

Batch Cooking: Prepare extra portions and store leftovers in the refrigerator for quick meals.
Customization: Add other toddler-friendly vegetables like carrots or sweet potatoes for variety.
Portable Meal: This dish is great for on-the-go meals or picnics.

Storage Information:

Refrigerator: Store the prepared salmon and green beans in an airtight container for up to 2 days. Reheat gently in the oven or microwave.

Instructions:

1. **Prepare the Ingredients:**
Preheat the oven to 375°F (190°C).
Trim and cut the green beans into bite-sized pieces.
Mince the garlic if using.
2. **Season the Salmon:**
Place the salmon fillet on a baking sheet lined with parchment paper.
Drizzle the salmon with half of the olive oil and lemon juice.
Sprinkle with dried dill, salt, pepper, and minced garlic if using.
3. **Prepare the Green Beans:**
In a medium bowl, toss the green beans with the remaining olive oil, salt, and pepper.
4. **Bake:**
Arrange the green beans around the salmon on the baking sheet.
Bake in the preheated oven for about 15-20 minutes, or until the salmon is cooked through and flakes easily with a fork, and the green beans are tender.
5. **Serve:**
Allow the salmon and green beans to cool slightly before serving to your toddler. Flake the salmon into small, manageable pieces if needed.

Nutritional Value per Serving (Approximate):

Calories: 220 Proteins: 20g Fats: 12g Carbohydrates: 8g

15 Minutes

30 Minutes

2 servings

Meatballs and Spaghetti

Ingredients:

For the Meatballs:
- 1/2 pound ground beef or turkey
- 1/4 cup breadcrumbs (whole wheat or panko)
- 1 egg
- 1/4 cup grated Parmesan cheese
- 1 small carrot, grated
- 1 clove garlic, minced
- 1/2 teaspoon dried oregano
- A pinch of salt and pepper (optional)
- 1 tablespoon olive oil (for cooking)

For the Sauce:
- 1 tablespoon olive oil
- 1/2 small onion, finely chopped
- 1 clove garlic, minced
- 1 can (14.5 ounces) diced tomatoes (no salt added)
- 1/2 teaspoon dried basil or oregano
- A pinch of salt and pepper (optional)

For the Spaghetti:
- One cup of tiny pasta forms, such macaroni or tiny shells
- Grated Parmesan cheese (optional, for serving)
- Fresh basil or parsley for garnish (optional)

Practical Tips for Preparing and Planning Meals:

Batch Cooking: *Make a larger batch of meatballs and store leftovers in the refrigerator or freezer for quick meals.*
Customization: *Add finely chopped vegetables like spinach or bell peppers to the sauce for extra nutrition.*
Portable Meal: *This dish is great for on-the-go meals or lunchboxes.*

Storage Information:

Refrigerator: *Store the prepared meatballs and sauce in an airtight container for up to 3 days. Store the cooked pasta separately to prevent it from becoming mushy. Reheat gently on the stovetop or in the microwave.*
Freezer: *Freeze the cooked meatballs and sauce in an airtight container for up to 1 month. Thaw in the refrigerator overnight before reheating.*

Instructions:

Prepare the Meatballs:
1. **Mix the Ingredients:**
In a large bowl, combine the ground beef or turkey, breadcrumbs, egg, grated Parmesan cheese, grated carrot, minced garlic, dried oregano, salt, and pepper (if using).
Mix well until all ingredients are evenly combined.
2. **Form the Meatballs:**
Shape the mixture into small meatballs, about 1-inch in diameter.
3. **Cook the Meatballs:**
Heat the olive oil in a large skillet over medium heat.
Add the meatballs to the skillet and cook for about 8-10 minutes, turning occasionally, until the meatballs are browned on all sides and cooked through.
Remove the meatballs from the skillet and set aside.

Prepare the Sauce:
1. **Sauté the Aromatics:**
In the same skillet, heat the olive oil over medium heat.
Add the chopped onion and garlic. Sauté for about 5 minutes, or until the onion is soft and translucent.
2. **Cook the Tomatoes:**
Add the diced tomatoes (with their juice) to the skillet. Stir in the dried basil or oregano and bring to a simmer. Cook for about 10 minutes, until the sauce has thickened slightly.
Add a pinch of salt and pepper if desired.
3. **Combine the Meatballs and Sauce:**
Return the cooked meatballs to the skillet with the sauce.
Stir gently to coat the meatballs with the sauce and heat through.

Prepare the Spaghetti:
1. **Cook the Pasta:**
Bring a large pot of water to a boil. Add the pasta and cook according to package instructions.
Drain the pasta and set aside.

Serve:
1. **Combine and Serve:**
In a large bowl, combine the cooked pasta with the meatballs and sauce.
Serve immediately, topped with grated Parmesan cheese and fresh basil or parsley if desired.
Allow the dish to cool slightly before serving to your toddler. Cut the meatballs into small, manageable pieces if needed.

Nutritional Value per Serving (Approximate):

Calories: 300 Proteins: 18g Fats: 12g Carbohydrates: 28g

15 Minutes

40 Minutes

2 servings

Turkey Meatloaf

Ingredients:

- ·1/2 pound ground turkey
- ·1/4 cup breadcrumbs (whole wheat or panko)
- ·1 small carrot, grated
- ·1 small zucchini, grated
- ·1/4 cup finely chopped onion
- ·1 clove garlic, minced (optional)
- ·1 egg, lightly beaten
- ·1/4 cup grated Parmesan cheese
- ·1 tablespoon ketchup (optional)
- ·1 teaspoon dried thyme (optional)
- ·A pinch of salt and pepper (optional)

Practical Tips for Preparing and Planning Meals:

Batch Cooking: Make a larger meatloaf and store leftovers in the refrigerator or freezer for quick meals.
Customization: Add finely chopped herbs like parsley or basil for extra flavor. You can also add other grated vegetables like bell peppers or spinach.
Texture Variety: For a smoother texture, finely chop all the vegetables or use a food processor.

Storage Information:

Refrigerator: Store the prepared meatloaf in an airtight container for up to 3 days. Reheat gently in the oven or microwave.
Freezer: Freeze the cooked meatloaf in individual portions in airtight containers for up to 1 month. Thaw in the refrigerator overnight before reheating.

Instructions:

1. **Preheat the Oven:**
Preheat your oven to 375°F (190°C).
2. **Prepare the Vegetables:**
Peel and grate the carrot.
Grate the zucchini.
Finely chop the onion and mince the garlic (if using).
3. **Mix the Ingredients:**
In a large bowl, combine the ground turkey, breadcrumbs, grated carrot, grated zucchini, chopped onion, minced garlic (if using), beaten egg, grated Parmesan cheese, ketchup (if using), dried thyme, salt, and pepper.
Mix well until all ingredients are evenly combined.
4. **Shape the Meatloaf:**
Transfer the mixture to a small loaf pan and press it down evenly. Alternatively, shape the mixture into a loaf shape and place it on a baking sheet lined with parchment paper.
5. **Bake the Meatloaf:**
Bake in the preheated oven for about 35-40 minutes, or until the meatloaf is cooked through and reaches an internal temperature of 165°F (74°C).
6. **Serve:**
Allow the meatloaf to cool slightly before slicing it into small, manageable pieces for your toddler.

Nutritional Value per Serving (Approximate):

Calories: 200 Proteins: 18g Fats: 8g Carbohydrates: 12g

10 Minutes

15 Minutes

2 servings

Fish Tacos

Ingredients:

·1 small fish fillet (such as cod or tilapia), about 4 ounces
·1 tablespoon olive oil
·1/2 teaspoon cumin
·1/2 teaspoon paprika
·A pinch of salt and pepper (optional)
·2 small whole wheat tortillas
·1/2 cup shredded lettuce
·1/4 cup grated carrot
·1/4 cup diced cucumber
·1/4 cup plain Greek yogurt or sour cream
·1 tablespoon lemon or lime juice
·1 tablespoon finely chopped fresh cilantro (optional)

Practical Tips for Preparing and Planning Meals:

Batch Cooking: Prepare extra fish and store leftovers in the refrigerator for quick meals.
Customization: Add other toddler-friendly vegetables like diced tomatoes or avocado for variety.
Portable Meal: These tacos are great for on-the-go meals or lunchboxes.

Storage Information:

Refrigerator: Store the cooked fish and prepared vegetables separately in airtight containers for up to 2 days. Reheat the fish gently in the microwave or oven before assembling the tacos.

Instructions:

1. **Prepare the Fish:**
Preheat the oven to 375°F (190°C).
Place the fish fillet on a baking sheet lined with parchment paper.
Drizzle the fish with olive oil and sprinkle with cumin, paprika, salt, and pepper (if using).
2. **Cook the Fish:**
Bake the fish in the preheated oven for about 12-15 minutes, or until the fish is cooked through and flakes easily with a fork.
3. **Prepare the Toppings:**
While the fish is cooking, wash and shred the lettuce, grate the carrot, and dice the cucumber.
In a small bowl, mix the Greek yogurt or sour cream with the lemon or lime juice and chopped cilantro (if using).
4. **Assemble the Tacos:**
Warm the whole wheat tortillas in the microwave for about 20 seconds or in a dry skillet for about 1 minute on each side.
Flake the cooked fish into small pieces and divide it between the tortillas.
Top each tortilla with shredded lettuce, grated carrot, and diced cucumber.
Drizzle the yogurt or sour cream mixture over the top.
5. **Serve:**
Allow the tacos to cool slightly before serving to your toddler. Cut the tacos into small, manageable pieces if needed.

Nutritional Value per Serving (Approximate):
Calories: 200 Proteins: 15g Fats: 8g Carbohydrates: 18g

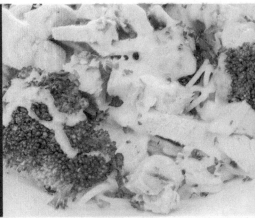

10 Minutes

20 Minutes

2 servings

Chicken and Broccoli Alfredo

Ingredients:

·1 small boneless, skinless chicken breast (about 4 ounces), diced
·One cup of tiny pasta forms, such macaroni or tiny shells
·1 cup small pasta shapes (such as mini shells or macaroni)
·1 cup broccoli florets, chopped
·1 tablespoon olive oil
·1 clove garlic, minced (optional)
·1/2 cup heavy cream
·1/4 cup grated Parmesan cheese
·1/2 cup chicken broth (low sodium)
·A pinch of salt and pepper (optional)
·Fresh parsley for garnish (optional)

Practical Tips for Preparing and Planning Meals:

Batch Cooking: Prepare a larger batch and store leftovers in the refrigerator for quick meals.
Customization: Add other toddler-friendly vegetables like peas or carrots for extra nutrition.
Texture Variety: For a smoother texture, finely chop all the vegetables.

Storage Information:

Refrigerator: Store the prepared Chicken and Broccoli Alfredo in an airtight container for up to 3 days. Reheat gently on the stovetop or in the microwave.
Freezer: Portion the dish into small, airtight containers and freeze for up to 1 month. Thaw in the refrigerator overnight before reheating.

Instructions:

1. **Cook the Pasta and Broccoli:**
Bring a large pot of water to a boil. Add the pasta and cook according to the package instructions.
In the last 3 minutes of the pasta cooking time, add the broccoli florets to the boiling water with the pasta.
Drain the pasta and broccoli and set aside.
2. **Cook the Chicken:**
While the pasta is cooking, heat the olive oil in a large skillet over medium heat.
Add the diced chicken and cook until browned and cooked through, about 5-7 minutes. Remove the chicken from the skillet and set aside.
3. **Make the Alfredo Sauce:**
In the same skillet, add the minced garlic (if using) and sauté for about 1 minute until fragrant.
Add the heavy cream and chicken broth to the skillet, stirring well to combine.
Bring the mixture to a simmer and cook for about 3-5 minutes, or until the sauce begins to thicken slightly.
Stir in the grated Parmesan cheese and continue to cook until the cheese is melted and the sauce is creamy.
Add a pinch of salt and pepper if desired.
4. **Combine and Serve:**
Return the cooked chicken, pasta, and broccoli to the skillet with the Alfredo sauce.
Stir gently to coat everything evenly with the sauce.
Allow the dish to cool slightly before serving to your toddler.
Garnish with fresh parsley if desired.

Nutritional Value per Serving (Approximate):

Calories: 250 Proteins: 18g Fats: 10g Carbohydrates: 22g

Turkey and Veggie Stir-Fry

Ingredients:

- 1/2 pound ground turkey
- 1 tablespoon olive oil
- 1 small carrot, peeled and thinly sliced
- 1 small bell pepper, diced
- 1 small zucchini, diced
- 1/2 cup broccoli florets, chopped
- 1 clove garlic, minced (optional)
- 1 tablespoon low-sodium soy sauce or tamari
- 1 teaspoon honey or maple syrup (optional)
- 1/2 teaspoon dried ginger or 1 teaspoon fresh grated ginger (optional)
- 1/4 cup low-sodium chicken broth or water
- 1 cup cooked rice or small pasta shapes (for serving)

Practical Tips for Preparing and Planning Meals:

Batch Cooking: Prepare a larger batch and store leftovers in the refrigerator or freezer for quick meals.

Customization: Add other toddler-friendly vegetables like snap peas, mushrooms, or spinach for variety.

Texture Variety: For a smoother texture, finely chop all the vegetables.

Storage Information:

Refrigerator: Store the prepared stir-fry in an airtight container for up to 3 days. Reheat gently on the stovetop or in the microwave.

Freezer: Portion the stir-fry into small, airtight containers and freeze for up to 1 month. Thaw in the refrigerator overnight before reheating.

Instructions:

1. **Prepare the Ingredients:**
Peel and thinly slice the carrot.
Dice the bell pepper and zucchini.
Chop the broccoli into small florets.
Mince the garlic (if using).

2. **Cook the Turkey:**
In a large skillet or wok, heat the olive oil over medium heat.
Add the ground turkey and cook until browned and cooked through, about 5-7 minutes. Break up the turkey into small pieces as it cooks.
Remove the cooked turkey from the skillet and set aside.

3. **Cook the Vegetables:**
In the same skillet, add the sliced carrot, diced bell pepper, diced zucchini, and chopped broccoli.
Cook for about 5 minutes, stirring occasionally, until the vegetables are tender but still crisp.

4. **Combine Turkey and Vegetables:**
Return the cooked turkey to the skillet with the vegetables.
Add the minced garlic (if using), soy sauce or tamari, honey or maple syrup (if using), and dried or fresh ginger (if using).
Pour in the chicken broth or water and stir well to combine.

5. **Simmer:**
Let the mixture simmer for about 3 minutes, or until the sauce has slightly thickened and everything is heated through.

6. **Serve:**
Allow the stir-fry to cool slightly before serving to your toddler.
Serve over cooked rice or small pasta shapes.

Nutritional Value per Serving (Approximate):

Calories: 180 Proteins: 16g Fats: 6g Carbohydrates: 18g

10 Minutes

25 Minutes

2 servings

Baked Cod with Sweet Potato Fries

Ingredients:

For the Baked Cod:
·1 small cod fillet (about 4 ounces)
·1 tablespoon olive oil
·1/2 teaspoon dried thyme or parsley
·1/2 teaspoon paprika
·A pinch of salt and pepper (optional)
·Lemon wedges for serving (optional)

For the Sweet Potato Fries:
·1 medium sweet potato, peeled and cut into thin strips
·1 tablespoon olive oil
·1/2 teaspoon paprika
·A pinch of salt (optional)

Practical Tips for Preparing and Planning Meals:

Batch Cooking: Prepare extra sweet potato fries and store leftovers in the refrigerator for quick snacks or meals.
Customization: Use other toddler-friendly fish like tilapia or haddock if preferred.
Texture Variety: For a smoother texture, mash the sweet potatoes after baking.

Storage Information:

Refrigerator: Store the prepared cod and sweet potato fries in separate airtight containers for up to 2 days. Reheat gently in the oven or microwave.
Freezer: Freeze the cooked sweet potato fries in a single layer on a baking sheet, then transfer to an airtight container and freeze for up to 1 month. Thaw in the refrigerator overnight before reheating.

Instructions:

1. **Prepare the Sweet Potato Fries:**
Preheat the oven to 400°F (200°C).
Peel and cut the sweet potato into thin strips.
In a bowl, toss the sweet potato strips with olive oil, paprika, and a pinch of salt if using.
Spread the sweet potato strips in a single layer on a baking sheet lined with parchment paper.
Bake for about 20-25 minutes, turning halfway through, until the fries are golden brown and crispy.

2. **Prepare the Baked Cod:**
While the sweet potato fries are baking, place the cod fillet on a separate baking sheet lined with parchment paper.
Drizzle the cod with olive oil and sprinkle with dried thyme or parsley, paprika, salt, and pepper if using.
Bake in the preheated oven (alongside the sweet potato fries) for about 12-15 minutes, or until the cod is cooked through and flakes easily with a fork.

3. **Serve:**
Allow the cod and sweet potato fries to cool slightly before serving to your toddler.
Serve the baked cod with a side of sweet potato fries and lemon wedges for squeezing over the fish if desired.

Nutritional Value per Serving (Approximate):

Calories: 220 Proteins: 20g Fats: 8g Carbohydrates: 18g

10 Minutes

30 Minutes

2 servings

Spaghetti Bolognese

Ingredients:

- 1/2 pound ground beef or turkey
- 1 tablespoon olive oil
- 1/2 small onion, finely chopped
- 1 small carrot, peeled and grated
- 1 small zucchini, grated
- 1 clove garlic, minced (optional)
- 1 can (14.5 ounces) diced tomatoes (no salt added)
- 1/4 cup tomato paste
- 1/2 teaspoon dried oregano
- 1/2 teaspoon dried basil
- A pinch of salt and pepper (optional)
- One cup of tiny pasta forms, such macaroni or tiny shells or spaghetti broken into small pieces
- Grated Parmesan cheese (optional, for serving)
- Fresh basil or parsley for garnish (optional)

Practical Tips for Preparing and Planning Meals:

Batch Cooking: Prepare a larger batch and store leftovers in the refrigerator or freezer for quick meals.
Customization: Add other finely chopped vegetables like bell peppers or spinach for extra nutrition.
Texture Variety: For a smoother texture, finely chop all the vegetables or use a food processor.

Storage Information:

Refrigerator: Store the prepared Bolognese sauce and pasta in separate airtight containers for up to 3 days. Reheat gently on the stovetop or in the microwave.
Freezer: Portion the Bolognese sauce into small, airtight containers and freeze for up to 1 month. Thaw in the refrigerator overnight before reheating.

Instructions:

1. **Cook the Pasta:**
Bring a large pot of water to a boil. Add the pasta and cook according to package instructions.
Drain the pasta and set aside.
2. **Prepare the Bolognese Sauce:**
In a large skillet or saucepan, heat the olive oil over medium heat.
Add the finely chopped onion and sauté for about 3-5 minutes, until softened.
Add the grated carrot, grated zucchini, and minced garlic (if using). Cook for another 2-3 minutes, stirring occasionally.
Add the ground beef or turkey to the skillet. Cook until browned and cooked through, breaking up the meat into small pieces with a spoon, about 5-7 minutes.
Stir in the diced tomatoes and tomato paste.
Add the dried oregano, dried basil, salt, and pepper (if using).
Bring the mixture to a simmer and cook for about 15 minutes, until the sauce has thickened slightly.
3. **Combine and Serve:**
Add the cooked pasta to the skillet with the Bolognese sauce. Stir gently to combine.
Allow the dish to cool slightly before serving to your toddler.
Serve topped with grated Parmesan cheese and fresh basil or parsley if desired.

Nutritional Value per Serving (Approximate):

Calories: 250 Proteins: 15g Fats: 10g Carbohydrates: 25g

10 Minutes

20 Minutes

2 servings

Chicken and Rice Pilaf

Ingredients:

- ·1 small boneless, skinless chicken breast (about 4 ounces), diced
- ·1 tablespoon olive oil
- ·1/2 small onion, finely chopped
- ·1 small carrot, peeled and diced
- ·1/2 cup frozen peas
- ·1/2 cup long-grain rice
- ·1 cup low-sodium chicken broth
- ·1/4 teaspoon dried thyme (optional)
- ·A pinch of salt and pepper (optional)
- ·Fresh parsley for garnish (optional)

Practical Tips for Preparing and Planning Meals:

Batch Cooking: Prepare a larger batch and store leftovers in the refrigerator for quick meals.

Customization: Add other toddler-friendly vegetables like bell peppers or zucchini for extra nutrition.

Texture Variety: For a smoother texture, finely chop all the vegetables.

Storage Information:

Refrigerator: Store the prepared chicken and rice pilaf in an airtight container for up to 3 days. Reheat gently on the stovetop or in the microwave.

Freezer: Portion the pilaf into small, airtight containers and freeze for up to 1 month. Thaw in the refrigerator overnight before reheating.

Instructions:

1. **Prepare the Ingredients:**
Dice the chicken breast into small, bite-sized pieces.
Peel and dice the carrot.
Finely chop the onion.

2. **Cook the Chicken:**
In a large skillet or saucepan, heat the olive oil over medium heat.
Add the diced chicken and cook until browned and cooked through, about 5-7 minutes. Remove the chicken from the skillet and set aside.

3. **Cook the Vegetables:**
In the same skillet, add the chopped onion and diced carrot. Sauté for about 3-5 minutes, until the vegetables are softened.

4. **Add the Rice and Broth:**
Stir in the rice and cook for about 1 minute to toast it slightly.
Add the low-sodium chicken broth, dried thyme (if using), and a pinch of salt and pepper (if desired).
Bring the mixture to a boil, then reduce the heat to low. Cover and simmer for about 15 minutes, or until the rice is tender and the liquid is absorbed.

5. **Combine and Serve:**
Add the cooked chicken and frozen peas to the skillet. Stir to combine and heat through. Allow the pilaf to cool slightly before serving to your toddler.
Garnish with fresh parsley if desired.

Nutritional Value per Serving (Approximate):
Calories: 220 Proteins: 15g Fats: 7g Carbohydrates: 25g

15 Minutes

20 Minutes

2 servings

Homemade Fish Sticks

Ingredients:

·1 small fish fillet (such as cod or tilapia), about 4 ounces
·1/4 cup whole wheat flour
·1 large egg, beaten
·1/2 cup breadcrumbs (whole wheat or panko)
·1/4 teaspoon garlic powder (optional)
·1/4 teaspoon paprika (optional)
·A pinch of salt and pepper (optional)
·2 tablespoons olive oil or cooking spray

Practical Tips for Preparing and Planning Meals:

Batch Cooking: Prepare extra fish sticks and store leftovers in the refrigerator or freezer for quick meals.
Customization: Add finely grated Parmesan cheese or dried herbs to the breadcrumb mixture for extra flavor.
Texture Variety: For a smoother texture, finely chop the fish before breading.

Storage Information:

Refrigerator: Store the cooked fish sticks in an airtight container for up to 2 days. Reheat gently in the oven or microwave.
Freezer: Freeze the cooked fish sticks in a single layer on a baking sheet, then transfer to an airtight container and freeze for up to 1 month. Thaw in the refrigerator overnight before reheating.

Instructions:

1. **Prepare the Fish:**
Preheat the oven to 400°F (200°C). A baking sheet can be lightly oiled with olive oil or lined with parchment paper.
Cut the fish fillet into small, toddler-friendly strips.
2. **Set Up the Breading Station:**
Place the flour in a shallow bowl.
Beat the egg in another shallow bowl.
In a third shallow bowl, mix the breadcrumbs with garlic powder, paprika, salt, and pepper if using.
3. **Bread the Fish:**
Dredge each fish strip in the flour, shaking off any excess.
Dip the fish strip into the beaten egg, allowing any excess to drip off.
Roll the fish strip in the breadcrumb mixture, pressing gently to ensure it is well-coated.
4. **Bake the Fish Sticks:**
Arrange the breaded fish strips on the prepared baking sheet.
Drizzle with olive oil or lightly spray with cooking spray.
Bake in the preheated oven for about 15-20 minutes, turning halfway through, until the fish sticks are golden brown and cooked through.
5. **Serve:**
Allow the fish sticks to cool slightly before serving to your toddler. Serve with a side of steamed vegetables or a dipping sauce like yogurt or applesauce.

Nutritional Value per Serving (Approximate):

Calories: 180 Proteins: 15g Fats: 6g Carbohydrates: 15g

20 Minutes

40 Minutes

4 servings

Chicken Lasagna

Ingredients:

For the Chicken Mixture:
- 1 small boneless, skinless chicken breast (about 4 ounces), cooked and shredded
- 1 small onion, finely chopped
- 1 clove garlic, minced
- 1 cup chopped spinach or finely grated carrot
- 1 can (14.5 ounces) diced tomatoes (no salt added)
- 1/2 teaspoon dried basil
- 1/2 teaspoon dried oregano
- 1 tablespoon olive oil
- A pinch of salt and pepper (optional)

For the Cheese Mixture:
- 1 cup ricotta cheese
- 1/2 cup grated Parmesan cheese
- 1 large egg
- 1/2 teaspoon dried parsley

For Assembly:
- 6-8 whole wheat lasagna noodles, cooked according to package instructions
- 1 cup shredded mozzarella cheese

Practical Tips for Preparing and Planning Meals:

Batch Cooking: Prepare a larger batch and store leftovers in the refrigerator or freezer for quick meals.
Customization: Add other finely chopped vegetables like bell peppers or zucchini for extra nutrition.
Texture Variety: For a smoother texture, finely chop all the vegetables or use a food processor.

Storage Information:

Refrigerator: Store the prepared lasagna in an airtight container for up to 3 days. Reheat gently in the oven or microwave.
Freezer: Portion the lasagna into small, airtight containers and freeze for up to 1 month. Thaw in the refrigerator overnight before reheating.

Instructions:

1. **Prepare the Chicken Mixture:**
In a large skillet, heat the olive oil over medium heat.
Add the chopped onion and garlic and sauté for about 3-5 minutes until softened.
Add the chopped spinach or grated carrot and cook for another 2-3 minutes.
Stir in the diced tomatoes, dried basil, and dried oregano. Simmer for about 10 minutes until the mixture thickens slightly.
Add the shredded chicken to the skillet and stir to combine. Season with a pinch of salt and pepper if desired. Set aside.

2. **Prepare the Cheese Mixture:**
In a medium bowl, combine the ricotta cheese, grated Parmesan cheese, egg, and dried parsley. Mix well.

3. **Assemble the Lasagna:**
Preheat the oven to 375°F (190°C).
Spread a small amount of the chicken mixture on the bottom of a baking dish.
Place a layer of cooked lasagna noodles over the chicken mixture.
Spread half of the cheese mixture over the noodles.
Add another layer of noodles, followed by a layer of the chicken mixture.
Repeat the layers, ending with a layer of the chicken mixture on top.
Sprinkle the shredded mozzarella cheese over the top layer.

4. **Bake the Lasagna:**
Cover the baking dish with aluminum foil and bake in the preheated oven for 20 minutes.
Remove the foil and bake for an additional 10-15 minutes until the cheese is melted and bubbly.

5. **Serve:**
Allow the lasagna to cool slightly before cutting it into small, manageable pieces for your toddler.

Nutritional Value per Serving (Approximate):

Calories: 280 Proteins: 18g Fats: 10g Carbohydrates: 30g

HEALTHY
DIETARY RECIPES

15 Minutes

25 Minutes

4 servings

Baked Veggie Tots

Ingredients:

- ·1 cup grated zucchini (about 1 medium zucchini)
- ·1 cup grated carrot (about 2 small carrots)
- ·1 small potato, peeled and grated
- ·1/4 cup finely chopped onion
- ·1/4 cup grated Parmesan cheese (or nutritional yeast for vegan)
- ·1/4 cup gluten-free breadcrumbs (or regular breadcrumbs if not gluten-free)
- ·1 large egg (or flax egg for vegan: 1 tablespoon ground flaxseed mixed with 3 tablespoons water, let sit for 5 minutes)
- ·1/2 teaspoon garlic powder
- ·1/2 teaspoon onion powder
- ·1/2 teaspoon dried parsley
- ·A pinch of salt and pepper
- ·Olive oil or cooking spray for greasing

Practical Tips for Preparing and Planning Meals:

Batch Cooking: Prepare a larger batch and store leftovers in the refrigerator or freezer for quick snacks or meals.
Customization: Add other grated vegetables like sweet potato or butternut squash for variety.
Portable Snack: These veggie tots are great for on-the-go snacks or lunchboxes.

Storage Information:

Refrigerator: Store the prepared veggie tots in an airtight container for up to 3 days. Reheat gently in the oven or microwave.
Freezer: Freeze the cooked veggie tots in a single layer on a baking sheet, then transfer to an airtight container and freeze for up to 1 month. Reheat in the oven until heated through and crispy.

Instructions:

1. **Preheat the Oven:**
Preheat your oven to 400°F (200°C). A baking sheet can be lightly oiled with olive oil or lined with parchment paper.
2. **Prepare the Vegetables:**
Grate the zucchini, carrot, and potato. Use a clean kitchen towel or cheesecloth to squeeze out any excess moisture from the grated vegetables. This will help the tots hold their shape and not become too soggy.
3. **Mix the Ingredients:**
In a large bowl, combine the grated zucchini, grated carrot, grated potato, finely chopped onion, grated Parmesan cheese (or nutritional yeast), gluten-free breadcrumbs, egg (or flax egg), garlic powder, onion powder, dried parsley, salt, and pepper. Mix well until all ingredients are evenly combined.
4. **Form the Tots:**
Scoop out small portions of the mixture and shape them into tot shapes using your hands. Place the shaped tots on the prepared baking sheet.
5. **Bake the Veggie Tots:**
Lightly spray or brush the tops of the tots with olive oil.
Bake in the preheated oven for about 20-25 minutes, turning halfway through, until the tots are golden brown and crispy on the outside.
6. **Serve:**
Allow the veggie tots to cool slightly before serving to your toddler. Serve with a side of ketchup, hummus, or dairy-free yogurt for dipping.

Nutritional Value per Serving (Approximate):

Calories: 80 Proteins: 2g Fats: 3g Carbohydrates: 10g

10 Minutes

15 Minutes

4 servings

Pumpkin Waffles

Ingredients:

·1 cup whole wheat flour (or gluten-free flour blend for gluten-free)
·1/2 cup pumpkin puree (canned or homemade)
·1/2 cup almond milk (or any plant-based milk)
·1 large egg (or flax egg for vegan: 1 tablespoon ground flaxseed mixed with 3 tablespoons water, let sit for 5 minutes)
·2 tablespoons olive oil or melted coconut oil
·2 tablespoons maple syrup or agave syrup
·1 teaspoon baking powder
·1/2 teaspoon ground cinnamon
·1/4 teaspoon ground nutmeg (optional)
·1/4 teaspoon ground ginger (optional)
·1/4 teaspoon ground cloves (optional)
·1/2 teaspoon vanilla extract (optional)
·A pinch of salt

Practical Tips for Preparing and Planning Meals:

Batch Cooking: Prepare a larger batch and store leftovers in the refrigerator or freezer for quick breakfasts or snacks.
Customization: Add other mix-ins like chopped nuts, raisins, or dairy-free chocolate chips for variety.
Portable Snack: These waffles are great for on-the-go snacks or lunchboxes.

Storage Information:

Refrigerator: Store the prepared waffles in an airtight container for up to 3 days. Reheat gently in a toaster or oven.
Freezer: Freeze the cooked waffles in a single layer on a baking sheet, then transfer to an airtight container and freeze for up to 1 month. Toast or bake from frozen.

Instructions:

1. **Prepare the Wet Ingredients:**
In a large bowl, whisk together the pumpkin puree, almond milk, egg (or flax egg), olive oil or melted coconut oil, maple syrup or agave syrup, and vanilla extract (if using).
2. **Mix the Dry Ingredients:**
In another bowl, whisk together the whole wheat flour (or gluten-free flour blend), baking powder, ground cinnamon, ground nutmeg (if using), ground ginger (if using), ground cloves (if using), and a pinch of salt.
3. Combine Wet and Dry Ingredients:
Pour the wet ingredients into the bowl with the dry ingredients.
Stir until just combined. Do not overmix.
4. **Preheat the Waffle Iron:**
Preheat your waffle iron according to the manufacturer's instructions. Lightly grease it with cooking spray or a small amount of oil if necessary.
5. **Cook the Waffles:**
Pour the batter onto the preheated waffle iron, spreading it out evenly.
Cook according to the manufacturer's instructions, usually for about 3-5 minutes, or until the waffles are golden brown and cooked through.
6. **Serve:**
Allow the waffles to cool slightly before serving to your toddler.
Serve with fresh fruit, a drizzle of maple syrup, or a dollop of dairy-free yogurt if desired.

Nutritional Value per Serving (Approximate):

Calories: 80 Proteins: 2g Fats: 3g Carbohydrates: 10g

10 Minutes

15 Minutes

4 servings

Spinach Banana Waffles

Ingredients:

- 1 cup spinach leaves, packed
- 1 ripe banana
- 1 cup whole wheat flour (or gluten-free flour blend for gluten-free)
- 1/2 cup almond milk (or any plant-based milk)
- 1 large egg (or flax egg for vegan: 1 tablespoon ground flaxseed mixed with 3 tablespoons water, let sit for 5 minutes)
- 1 tablespoon olive oil or melted coconut oil
- 1 tablespoon maple syrup or agave syrup
- 1 teaspoon baking powder
- 1/2 teaspoon vanilla extract (optional)
- A pinch of salt

Practical Tips for Preparing and Planning Meals:

Batch Cooking: Prepare a larger batch and store leftovers in the refrigerator or freezer for quick breakfasts or snacks.
Customization: Add other mix-ins like blueberries, chocolate chips, or finely chopped nuts for variety.
Portable Snack: These waffles are great for on-the-go snacks or lunchboxes.

Storage Information:

Refrigerator: Store the prepared waffles in an airtight container for up to 3 days. Reheat gently in a toaster or oven.
Freezer: Freeze the cooked waffles in a single layer on a baking sheet, then transfer to an airtight container and freeze for up to 1 month. Toast or bake from frozen.

Instructions:

1. **Prepare the Wet Ingredients:**
In a blender, combine the spinach leaves, ripe banana, almond milk, egg (or flax egg), olive oil or melted coconut oil, maple syrup or agave syrup, and vanilla extract (if using). Blend until smooth.
2. **Mix the Dry Ingredients:**
In a large bowl, whisk together the whole wheat flour (or gluten-free flour blend), baking powder, and salt.
3. **Combine Wet and Dry Ingredients:**
Pour the spinach and banana mixture into the bowl with the dry ingredients.
Stir until just combined. Do not overmix.
4. **Preheat the Waffle Iron:**
Preheat your waffle iron according to the manufacturer's instructions. Lightly grease it with cooking spray or a small amount of oil if necessary.
5. **Cook the Waffles:**
Pour the batter onto the preheated waffle iron, spreading it out evenly.
Cook according to the manufacturer's instructions, usually for about 3-5 minutes, or until the waffles are golden brown and cooked through.
6. **Serve:**
Allow the waffles to cool slightly before serving to your toddler.
Serve with fresh fruit, a drizzle of maple syrup, or a dollop of dairy-free yogurt if desired.

Nutritional Value per Serving (Approximate):

Calories: 150 Proteins: 4g Fats: 5g Carbohydrates: 22g

20 Minutes

45 Minutes

4 servings

Vegan Lentil Lasagna

Ingredients:

For the Lentil Filling:
·1 cup dried green or brown lentils, rinsed and drained
·1 small onion, finely chopped
·2 cloves garlic, minced
·1 small carrot, grated
·1 small zucchini, grated
·1 can (14.5 ounces) diced tomatoes (no salt added)
·2 cups vegetable broth (low-sodium)
·1 teaspoon dried basil
·1 teaspoon dried oregano
·1 tablespoon olive oil
·A pinch of salt and pepper (optional)
For the Cheese Sauce:
·1 cup raw cashews (soaked in water for at least 4 hours or overnight)
·1/2 cup nutritional yeast
·1/2 cup unsweetened almond milk (or any plant-based milk)
·2 tablespoons lemon juice
·1 clove garlic
·A pinch of salt
For Assembly:
·6-8 whole wheat or gluten-free lasagna noodles, cooked according to package instructions
·1 cup fresh spinach, chopped

Practical Tips for Preparing and Planning Meals:

Batch Cooking: Prepare a larger batch and store leftovers in the refrigerator or freezer for quick meals.
Customization: Add other finely chopped vegetables like bell peppers or mushrooms for extra nutrition.
Texture Variety: For a smoother texture, blend the lentil filling slightly.

Storage Information:

Refrigerator: Store the prepared lasagna in an airtight container for up to 3 days. Reheat gently in the oven or microwave.
Freezer: Freeze the lasagna in individual portions in airtight containers for up to 1 month. Thaw in the refrigerator overnight before reheating.

Instructions:

1. **Prepare the Lentil Filling:**
In a large pot, heat the olive oil over medium heat. Add the chopped onion and garlic, and sauté for about 3-5 minutes until softened.
Add the grated carrot and zucchini, and cook for another 3 minutes.
Stir in the rinsed lentils, diced tomatoes, vegetable broth, dried basil, and dried oregano.
Bring to a boil, then reduce the heat to low and let it simmer for about 25-30 minutes, or until the mixture has thickened and the lentils are cooked. If preferred, season with salt and pepper.
2. **Prepare the Cheese Sauce:**
Drain and rinse the soaked cashews.
In a blender, combine the cashews, nutritional yeast, almond milk, lemon juice, garlic, and a pinch of salt.
Blend until smooth and creamy, adding more almond milk if needed to reach a pourable consistency.
3. **Assemble the Lasagna:**
Preheat your oven to 375°F (190°C).
Spread a small amount of the lentil filling on the bottom of a baking dish.
Place a layer of lasagna noodles over the filling. Spread a layer of lentil filling over the noodles, followed by a layer of chopped spinach.
Drizzle some of the cheese sauce over the spinach. Repeat the layers, ending with a layer of lentil filling and a generous drizzle of cheese sauce on top.
4. **Bake the Lasagna:**
Cover the baking dish with aluminum foil and bake in the preheated oven for 20 minutes.
Remove the foil and bake for an additional 10-15 minutes, or until the top is golden and bubbly.
5. **Serve:**
Allow the lasagna to cool slightly before cutting it into small, manageable pieces for your toddler.

Nutritional Value per Serving (Approximate):

Calories: 250 Proteins: 12g Fats: 6g Carbohydrates: 35g

10 Minutes

20 Minutes

2 servings

Dairy-Free Creamy Carrot Soup

Ingredients:

- 1 tablespoon olive oil
- 1 small onion, finely chopped
- 1 clove garlic, minced (optional)
- 4 large carrots, peeled and sliced
- 2 cups low-sodium vegetable broth
- 1/2 cup coconut milk (full-fat or light)
- 1/2 teaspoon ground ginger (optional)
- A pinch of salt and pepper (optional)
- Fresh parsley or chives for garnish (optional)

Practical Tips for Preparing and Planning Meals:

Batch Cooking: Prepare a larger batch and store leftovers in the refrigerator or freezer for quick meals.
Customization: Add other vegetables like sweet potatoes or parsnips for extra nutrition.
Texture Variety: For a smoother texture, strain the blended soup through a fine mesh sieve.

Storage Information:

Refrigerator: Store the prepared soup in an airtight container for up to 3 days. Reheat gently on the stovetop or in the microwave.
Freezer: Freeze the soup in small, airtight containers for up to 1 month. Thaw in the refrigerator overnight before reheating.

Instructions:

1. **Prepare the Vegetables:**
Peel and slice the carrots.
Finely chop the onion.
Mince the garlic if using.
2. **Cook the Vegetables:**
In a large pot, heat the olive oil over medium heat.
Add the chopped onion and garlic (if using).
Sauté for about 3-5 minutes, until the onion is soft and translucent.
Add the sliced carrots and cook for another 5 minutes, stirring occasionally.
3. **Add the Broth:**
Pour in the vegetable broth and bring the mixture to a boil.
Reduce the heat to low and let it simmer for about 15 minutes, or until the carrots are tender.
4. **Blend the Soup:**
Remove the pot from the heat and let it cool slightly.
Use an immersion blender to puree the soup until smooth. Alternatively, carefully transfer the soup to a blender and blend until smooth, then return it to the pot.
5. **Add the Coconut Milk:**
Stir in the coconut milk and ground ginger (if using).
Season with a pinch of salt and pepper if desired.
Heat the soup gently over low heat until warmed through.
6. **Serve:**
Allow the soup to cool slightly before serving to your toddler.
Garnish with fresh parsley or chives if desired.

Nutritional Value per Serving (Approximate):

Calories: 80 Proteins: 2g Fats: 3g Carbohydrates: 12g

15 Minutes

20 Minutes

12 servings

Gluten-Free Quinoa and Veggie Bites

Ingredients:

- 1 cup cooked quinoa
- 1/2 cup grated zucchini
- 1/2 cup grated carrot
- 1/4 cup finely chopped spinach
- 1/4 cup finely chopped onion
- 1 clove garlic, minced (optional)
- 1/4 cup gluten-free breadcrumbs
- 1/4 cup nutritional yeast (optional)
- 1 flax egg (1 tablespoon ground flaxseed mixed with 3 tablespoons water, let sit for 5 minutes)
- 1/2 teaspoon dried oregano
- 1/2 teaspoon dried basil
- A pinch of salt and pepper (optional)
- Olive oil or cooking spray for greasing

Practical Tips for Preparing and Planning Meals:

Batch Cooking: Prepare a larger batch and store leftovers in the refrigerator or freezer for quick snacks.

Customization: Add other finely chopped vegetables like bell peppers or sweet corn for extra nutrition.

Portable Snack: These bites are great for on-the-go snacks or lunchboxes.

Storage Information:

Refrigerator: Store the prepared bites in an airtight container for up to 3 days. Reheat gently in the oven or microwave.

Freezer: Freeze the cooked bites in a single layer on a baking sheet, then transfer to an airtight container and freeze for up to 1 month. Thaw in the refrigerator overnight before reheating.

Instructions:

1. **Prepare the Flax Egg:**
In a small bowl, combine the ground flaxseed with water. Stir well and let it sit for about 5 minutes until it thickens.

2. **Preheat the Oven:**
Preheat your oven to 375°F (190°C). Grease a mini muffin tin with olive oil or cooking spray.

3. **Prepare the Veggies:**
Grate the zucchini and carrot. Finely chop the spinach and onion. Mince the garlic if using.

4. **Combine the Ingredients:**
In a large bowl, combine the cooked quinoa, grated zucchini, grated carrot, chopped spinach, chopped onion, minced garlic (if using), gluten-free breadcrumbs, nutritional yeast (if using), dried oregano, dried basil, salt, and pepper.
Add the prepared flax egg and mix until all ingredients are well combined.

5. **Form the Bites:**
Scoop the mixture into the greased mini muffin tin, pressing down lightly to compact the mixture.

6. **Bake:**
Bake in the preheated oven for 15-20 minutes, or until the bites are golden brown and firm to the touch.

7. **Serve:**
Allow the quinoa and veggie bites to cool slightly before serving to your toddler.

Nutritional Value per Serving (Approximate):

Calories: 100 Proteins: 4g Fats: 3g Carbohydrates: 14g

15 Minutes

20 Minutes

2 servings

Vegan Chickpea Nuggets

Ingredients:

·1 can (15 ounces) chickpeas, rinsed and drained
·1 small carrot, peeled and grated
·1/4 cup finely chopped onion
·1 clove garlic, minced (optional)
·1/4 cup breadcrumbs (use gluten-free if needed)
·1 tablespoon nutritional yeast (optional)
·1 teaspoon ground cumin
·1/2 teaspoon paprika
·1/4 teaspoon turmeric (optional)
·1 tablespoon olive oil
·1 tablespoon ground flaxseed mixed with 3 tablespoons water (flax egg)
·A pinch of salt and pepper (optional)
·Olive oil or cooking spray for baking

Practical Tips for Preparing and Planning Meals:

Batch Cooking: Prepare a larger batch and store leftovers in the refrigerator or freezer for quick meals.
Customization: Add other finely chopped vegetables like bell peppers or spinach for extra nutrition.
·**Portable Snack:** These nuggets are great for on-the-go meals or lunchboxes.

Storage Information:

Refrigerator: Store the prepared nuggets in an airtight container for up to 3 days. Reheat gently in the oven or microwave.
Freezer: Freeze the cooked nuggets in a single layer on a baking sheet, then transfer to an airtight container and freeze for up to 1 month. Thaw in the refrigerator overnight before reheating.

Instructions:

1. **Prepare the Flax Egg:**
In a small bowl, combine the ground flaxseed with water. Stir well and let it sit for about 5 minutes until it thickens.
2. **Prepare the Chickpea Mixture:**
In a food processor, combine the chickpeas, grated carrot, chopped onion, minced garlic (if using), breadcrumbs, nutritional yeast (if using), ground cumin, paprika, turmeric (if using), olive oil, and the prepared flax egg. Pulse the mixture until it is well combined but still slightly chunky. You don't want it to be completely smooth.
3. **Form the Nuggets:**
Preheat your oven to 375°F (190°C) and grease a baking sheet lightly with some olive oil or grease it with parchment paper.
Take small portions of the chickpea mixture and shape them into nugget-sized patties. Place the nuggets on the prepared baking sheet.
4. **Bake the Nuggets:**
Lightly brush or spray the tops of the nuggets with olive oil.
Bake in the preheated oven for about 15-20 minutes, flipping halfway through, until the nuggets are golden brown and slightly crispy on the outside.
5. **Serve:**
Allow the nuggets to cool slightly before serving to your toddler. Serve with a dipping sauce like hummus, dairy-free yogurt, or ketchup.

Nutritional Value per Serving (Approximate):

Calories: 120 Proteins: 5g Fats: 4g Carbohydrates: 15g

5 Minutes

25 Minutes

2 servings

Dairy-Free Coconut Rice Pudding

Ingredients:

·1/2 cup jasmine rice
·1 can (13.5 ounces) coconut milk (full-fat or light)
·1/2 cup water
·2 tablespoons maple syrup or honey (optional, for toddlers over 1 year old)
·1 teaspoon vanilla extract
·A pinch of salt
·1/4 teaspoon ground cinnamon (optional)
·Fresh fruit for topping (optional)

Practical Tips for Preparing and Planning Meals:

Batch Cooking: Prepare a larger batch and store leftovers in the refrigerator for quick snacks or breakfasts.
Customization: Add finely chopped nuts, raisins, or a sprinkle of nutmeg for extra flavor and texture.
Portable Snack: This pudding can be stored in small containers for an easy on-the-go snack.

Storage Information:

Refrigerator: Store the prepared rice pudding in an airtight container for up to 3 days. Serve cold or reheat gently on the stovetop or in the microwave.
Freezer: Freeze the rice pudding in small, airtight containers for up to 1 month. Thaw in the refrigerator overnight before serving.

Instructions:

1. **Prepare the Rice:**
Rinse the jasmine rice under cold water until the water runs clear.
2. **Cook the Rice Pudding:**
In a medium saucepan, combine the rinsed rice, coconut milk, water, maple syrup or honey (if using), vanilla extract, and a pinch of salt.
Bring the mixture to a gentle boil over medium heat, stirring occasionally.
Once it reaches a boil, reduce the heat to low and let it simmer uncovered. Stir frequently to prevent the rice from sticking to the bottom of the pan.
Cook for about 20-25 minutes, or until the rice is tender and the pudding has thickened to your desired consistency. If it gets too thick, you can add a little more water or coconut milk to achieve the desired consistency.
3. **Add Cinnamon (Optional):**
Stir in the ground cinnamon if using.
4. **Serve:**
Allow the rice pudding to cool slightly before serving to your toddler.
Top with fresh fruit if desired.

Nutritional Value per Serving (Approximate):

Calories: 160 Proteins: 2g Fats: 7g Carbohydrates: 23g

15 Minutes

25 Minutes

2 servings

Vegan Sweet Potato and Black Bean Tacos

Ingredients:

·1 small sweet potato, peeled and diced
·1/2 cup black beans, cooked and drained
·1 tablespoon olive oil
·1/2 teaspoon ground cumin
·1/2 teaspoon paprika
·A pinch of salt and pepper (optional)
·1/2 avocado, diced
·1/4 cup finely chopped red bell pepper
·1/4 cup finely chopped red onion (optional)
·1 tablespoon chopped fresh cilantro (optional)
·2 small corn or whole wheat tortillas
·Lime wedges for serving (optional)

Practical Tips for Preparing and Planning Meals:

Batch Cooking: Prepare extra roasted sweet potatoes and black beans for quick meal assembly.
Customization: Add other toddler-friendly toppings like shredded lettuce, tomatoes, or a dollop of dairy-free yogurt.
Portable Meal: These tacos are great for on-the-go meals or lunchboxes.

Storage Information:

Refrigerator: Store the roasted sweet potatoes and black beans in separate airtight containers for up to 3 days. Reheat gently before assembling the tacos.
Freezer: Freeze the roasted sweet potatoes in an airtight container for up to 1 month. Thaw in the refrigerator overnight before reheating.

Instructions:

1. **Prepare the Sweet Potatoes:**
Preheat the oven to 400°F (200°C).
Peel and dice the sweet potato into small cubes.
In a bowl, toss the sweet potato cubes with olive oil, ground cumin, paprika, salt, and pepper if using.
Arrange the sugar snaps onto a baking tray covered with parchment paper, then bake for approximately 20 to 25 minutes, or until they are soft and have a hint of crunch.
2. **Prepare the Black Beans:**
While the sweet potatoes are baking, heat the black beans in a small saucepan over low heat until warmed through.
3. **Prepare the Toppings:**
Dice the avocado and finely chop the red bell pepper and red onion (if using). Chop the fresh cilantro.
4. **Assemble the Tacos:**
Warm the tortillas in a dry skillet or microwave for about 20 seconds.
Place a portion of the roasted sweet potatoes and black beans onto each tortilla. Top with diced avocado, chopped bell pepper, red onion (if using), and cilantro.
5. **Serve:**
Serve the tacos with lime wedges for squeezing over the top if desired.
Allow the tacos to cool slightly before serving to your toddler. Cut into small, manageable pieces if needed.

Nutritional Value per Serving (Approximate):

Calories: 200 Proteins: 5g Fats: 6g Carbohydrates: 34g

10 Minutes

15 Minutes

2 servings

Veggie Fried Rice

Ingredients:

·1 cup cooked rice (preferably chilled)
·1/2 cup frozen peas and carrots, thawed
·1/4 cup finely chopped bell pepper
·1/4 cup finely chopped onion
·1/4 cup finely chopped zucchini
·1 clove garlic, minced (optional)
·1 tablespoon soy sauce or tamari (for gluten-free)
·1 tablespoon olive oil or vegetable oil
·1/2 teaspoon sesame oil (optional)
·1 large egg (or scrambled tofu for vegan)
Fresh chopped green onions for garnish (optional)

Practical Tips for Preparing and Planning Meals:

Batch Cooking: Prepare a larger batch and store leftovers in the refrigerator for quick meals.
Customization: Add other toddler-friendly vegetables like corn, broccoli, or snap peas for variety.
Portable Meal: This fried rice is great for on-the-go meals or lunchboxes.

Storage Information:

Refrigerator: Store the prepared veggie fried rice in an airtight container for up to 3 days. Reheat gently in the skillet or microwave.
Freezer: Portion the fried rice into small, airtight containers and freeze for up to 1 month. Thaw in the refrigerator overnight before reheating.

Instructions:

1. **Prepare the Ingredients:**
Ensure the rice is cooked and chilled. Leftover rice works best for fried rice.
Thaw the frozen peas and carrots.
Finely chop the bell pepper, onion, and zucchini. Mince the garlic if using.
2. **Cook the Egg:**
In a large skillet or wok, heat 1 teaspoon of olive oil over medium heat.
Crack the egg into the skillet and scramble until fully cooked. Remove from the skillet and set aside. If using scrambled tofu, cook it in the same way.
3. **Cook the Vegetables:**
In the same skillet, heat the remaining olive oil over medium heat.
Add the chopped onion and garlic (if using). Sauté for about 2 minutes until the onion is translucent.
Add the bell pepper, zucchini, peas, and carrots. Cook for about 5 minutes, stirring occasionally, until the vegetables are tender.
4. **Add the Rice:**
Increase the heat to medium-high and add the chilled rice to the skillet.
Stir well to combine the rice with the vegetables. Cook for about 3-5 minutes, stirring frequently, until the rice is heated through and slightly crispy.
5. **Season the Fried Rice:**
Add the soy sauce or tamari and sesame oil (if using) to the skillet.
Stir well to evenly distribute the sauce. Add the scrambled egg (or tofu) back to the skillet and mix thoroughly.
6. **Serve:**
Remove from heat and allow the fried rice to cool slightly before serving to your toddler.
Garnish with fresh chopped green onions if desired.

Nutritional Value per Serving (Approximate):

Calories: 180 Proteins: 4g Fats: 4g Carbohydrates: 30g

SNACK AND
FINGER FOODS

10 Minutes

0 Minutes

2 servings

Pitta Bread Slices with Smashed Avocado

Ingredients:

·1 whole pitta bread (whole wheat or gluten-free)
·1 ripe avocado
·1 teaspoon lemon or lime juice
·A pinch of salt (optional)
·A pinch of pepper (optional)
·A pinch of paprika or cumin (optional, for flavor)
·Cherry tomatoes, halved (optional, for garnish)

Practical Tips for Preparing and Planning Meals:

Batch Preparation: Prepare the smashed avocado ahead of time and store it in an airtight container in the refrigerator for up to 1 day. Assemble just before serving.
Customization: Add other toppings like finely chopped herbs, a sprinkle of nutritional yeast, or thinly sliced radishes for variety.
Portable Snack: These pitta bread slices with smashed avocado are great for on-the-go snacks or lunchboxes.

Storage Information:

Refrigerator: Store the smashed avocado in an airtight container for up to 1 day. Store the pitta bread slices separately and assemble just before serving to keep them fresh.

Instructions:

1. **Prepare the Pitta Bread:**
Warm the pitta bread slightly in a toaster or oven. Once warmed, cut the pitta bread into small, toddler-friendly slices or wedges.
2. **Prepare the Avocado:**
Cut the ripe avocado in half, remove the pit, and scoop the flesh into a bowl.
Mash the avocado with a fork until smooth. Add lemon or lime juice and stir to combine. Season with a pinch of salt, pepper, and paprika or cumin if using.
3. **Assemble the Slices:**
Spread a generous amount of the smashed avocado onto each pitta bread slice. Top with halved cherry tomatoes if desired for added color and nutrition.
4. **Serve:**
Arrange the pitta bread slices with smashed avocado on a plate and serve immediately as a fun and nutritious snack for your toddler.

Nutritional Value per Serving (Approximate):

Calories: 140 Proteins: 4g Fats: 8g Carbohydrates: 16g

10 Minutes

0 Minutes

2 servings

Cheese and Pineapple Cubes

Ingredients:

·*1 cup fresh pineapple, cut into small cubes*
·*1 cup cheese (cheddar or your toddler's favorite), cut into small cubes*
·*Toothpicks or small skewers (optional)*

Practical Tips for Preparing and Planning Meals:

Batch Preparation: Cut the pineapple and cheese ahead of time and store them in separate airtight containers in the refrigerator.
Customization: Add other toddler-friendly fruits like grapes or melon cubes for variety.
Portable Snack: These cheese and pineapple cubes are great for on-the-go snacks or lunchboxes.

Storage Information:

Refrigerator: Store the prepared cheese and pineapple cubes in separate airtight containers for up to 2 days. Assemble just before serving to keep them fresh.

Instructions:

1. **Prepare the Pineapple:**
Cut the fresh pineapple into small, bite-sized cubes. If using canned pineapple, make sure to drain it well and cut it into appropriate sizes.
2. **Prepare the Cheese:**
Cut the cheese into small, bite-sized cubes.
3. **Assemble the Cubes:**
Pair one piece of pineapple with one piece of cheese. You can serve them as they are or assemble them on toothpicks or small skewers for easy handling.
4. **Serve:**
Arrange the cheese and pineapple cubes on a plate and serve immediately as a fun and nutritious snack for your toddler.

Nutritional Value per Serving (Approximate):
Calories: 90 Proteins: 5g Fats: 5g Carbohydrates: 8g

10 Minutes

0 Minutes

12 servings

Energy Balls

Ingredients:

·1 cup rolled oats (use gluten-free oats if needed)
·1/2 cup almond butter or peanut butter (or sunflower seed butter for nut-free option)
·1/4 cup honey or maple syrup (for vegan option)
·1/4 cup mini chocolate chips (dairy-free if needed) or raisins
·1/4 cup ground flaxseed or chia seeds
·1 teaspoon vanilla extract
·A pinch of salt (optional)
·1/4 cup shredded coconut (optional)

Practical Tips for Preparing and Planning Meals:

Batch Cooking: Prepare a larger batch and store leftovers in the refrigerator or freezer for quick snacks.
Customization: Add other toddler-friendly mix-ins like chopped nuts, seeds, or dried fruit for variety.
Portable Snack: These energy balls are great for on-the-go snacks or lunchboxes.

Storage Information:

Refrigerator: Store the prepared energy balls in an airtight container for up to 1 week.
Freezer: Freeze the energy balls in a single layer on a baking sheet, then transfer to an airtight container and freeze for up to 1 month. Thaw in the refrigerator before serving.

Instructions:

1. **Combine the Ingredients:**
In a large bowl, combine the rolled oats, almond butter or peanut butter, honey or maple syrup, mini chocolate chips or raisins, ground flaxseed or chia seeds, vanilla extract, and a pinch of salt if using.
Mix well until all the ingredients are evenly combined. If the mixture is too dry, add a little more honey or maple syrup. If it is too wet, add a bit more oats or flaxseed.
2. **Form the Balls:**
Using your hands, form the mixture into small balls, about 1 inch in diameter. You should get about 12 energy balls.
3. **Chill:**
Place the energy balls on a baking sheet lined with parchment paper and refrigerate for at least 30 minutes to help them firm up.
4. **Serve:**
Once chilled, the energy balls are ready to serve. Store any leftovers in an airtight container in the refrigerator.

Nutritional Value per Serving (Approximate):
Calories: 100 Proteins: 2g Fats: 5g Carbohydrates: 12g

10 Minutes

25 Minutes

2 servings

Sweet Potato Bites

Ingredients:

·1 large sweet potato, peeled and cut into bite-sized cubes
·1 tablespoon olive oil or coconut oil
·1/2 teaspoon ground cinnamon (optional)
·1/4 teaspoon ground nutmeg (optional)
·A pinch of salt (optional)
·1 tablespoon maple syrup or honey (optional for toddlers over 1 year old)

Practical Tips for Preparing and Planning Meals:

Batch Cooking: Prepare a larger batch and store leftovers in the refrigerator for quick snacks or meals.
Customization: Add other toddler-friendly seasonings like paprika or rosemary for variety.
Portable Snack: These sweet potato bites are great for on-the-go snacks or lunchboxes.

Storage Information:

Refrigerator: Store the prepared sweet potato bites in an airtight container for up to 3 days. Reheat gently in the oven or microwave.
Freezer: Freeze the cooked sweet potato bites in a single layer on a baking sheet, then transfer to an airtight container and freeze for up to 1 month. Reheat in the oven until heated through and crispy.

Instructions:

1. **Preheat the Oven:**
Preheat your oven to 400°F (200°C). Grease a baking sheet gently with coconut oil or some olive oil, or line it with parchment paper.
2. **Prepare the Sweet Potato:**
Peel the sweet potato and cut it into bite-sized cubes.
3. **Season the Sweet Potato:**
In a large bowl, toss the sweet potato cubes with olive oil or coconut oil, ground cinnamon, ground nutmeg, and a pinch of salt if using.
If desired, add maple syrup or honey and toss to coat evenly.
4. **Bake the Sweet Potato Bites:**
Spread the seasoned sweet potato cubes in a single layer on the prepared baking sheet. Bake in the preheated oven for 20-25 minutes, turning halfway through, until the sweet potatoes are tender and slightly crispy on the edges.
5. **Serve:**
Allow the sweet potato bites to cool slightly before serving to your toddler.

Nutritional Value per Serving (Approximate):
Calories: 90 Proteins: 1g Fats: 3g Carbohydrates: 15g

Banana Sushi

Ingredients:

·1 ripe banana
·2 tablespoons almond butter or peanut butter (or sunflower seed butter for nut-free option)
·1/4 cup granola or crushed cereal
·1 tablespoon raisins or dried cranberries (optional)
·1 tablespoon shredded coconut (optional)

Practical Tips for Preparing and Planning Meals:

Batch Cooking: Prepare the banana and toppings ahead of time and assemble just before serving.
Customization: Add other toddler-friendly toppings like chopped nuts, chia seeds, or chocolate chips for variety.
Portable Snack: This banana sushi is great for on-the-go snacks or lunchboxes.

Storage Information:

Refrigerator: Best served immediately, but can be stored in an airtight container for up to 1 day. Assemble the sushi just before serving to maintain freshness.

Instructions:

1. **Prepare the Banana:**
Peel the banana and place it on a flat surface.
2. **Add the Nut Butter:**
Spread a thin layer of almond butter or peanut butter evenly over the banana.
3. **Add Toppings:**
Sprinkle granola or crushed cereal over the nut butter.
Add raisins or dried cranberries and shredded coconut if using.
4. **Slice the Banana:**
Use a sharp knife to slice the banana into small rounds, about 1/2 inch thick, creating sushi-like pieces.
5. **Serve:**
Arrange the banana sushi pieces on a plate and serve immediately as a fun and nutritious snack for your toddler.

Nutritional Value per Serving (Approximate):

Calories: 120 Proteins: 2g Fats: 4g Carbohydrates: 22g

10 Minutes

0 Minutes

2 servings

Apple Sandwiches

Ingredients:

·1 large apple (any variety)
·2 tablespoons almond butter or peanut butter (or sunflower seed butter for nut-free option)
·2 tablespoons granola or oats
·1 tablespoon raisins or dried cranberries (optional)
·1 tablespoon shredded coconut (optional)
·A dash of cinnamon (optional)

Practical Tips for Preparing and Planning Meals:

Batch Cooking: Prepare the apple slices and filling ahead of time and assemble just before serving.
Customization: Add other toddler-friendly toppings like chopped nuts, chia seeds, or chocolate chips for variety.
Portable Snack: These apple sandwiches are great for on-the-go snacks or lunchboxes.

Storage Information:

Refrigerator: Store the apple slices in an airtight container for up to 1 day. Assemble the sandwiches just before serving to prevent the apple slices from browning.

Instructions:

1. **Prepare the Apple:**
Wash and core the apple.
Slice the apple into thin rounds, about 1/4 inch thick.
2. **Add the Filling:**
Spread a thin layer of almond butter or peanut butter on one side of each apple slice.
3. **Add Toppings:**
Sprinkle granola or oats over the nut butter. Add raisins or dried cranberries, shredded coconut, and a dash of cinnamon if using.
4.   Assemble the Sandwiches:
Place another apple slice on top of the filling to create a sandwich.
5.   **Serve:**
Serve immediately as a fun and nutritious snack for your toddler.

Nutritional Value per Serving (Approximate):
Calories: 100 Proteins: 2g Fats: 6g Carbohydrates: 12g

Mini Caprese Skewers

Ingredients:

·12 cherry tomatoes
·12 mini mozzarella balls (bocconcini)
·12 fresh basil leaves
·1 tablespoon olive oil
·1 tablespoon balsamic vinegar (optional)
·A pinch of salt and pepper (optional)
·12 small skewers or toothpicks

Practical Tips for Preparing and Planning Meals:

Batch Cooking: Prepare a larger batch and store leftovers in the refrigerator for quick snacks.
Customization: Add other toddler-friendly ingredients like cucumber slices or small pieces of bell pepper for variety.
Portable Snack: These mini skewers are great for on-the-go snacks or lunchboxes.

Storage Information:

Refrigerator: Store the prepared skewers in an airtight container for up to 1 day. For best results, add the olive oil and balsamic vinegar just before serving.

Instructions:

1. **Prepare the Ingredients:**
Wash the cherry tomatoes and fresh basil leaves.
Drain the mini mozzarella balls.
2. **Assemble the Skewers:**
Thread one cherry tomato, one mini mozzarella ball, and one fresh basil leaf onto each skewer or toothpick.
Repeat until all the ingredients are used.
3. **Season:**
Place the assembled skewers on a plate.
Drizzle with olive oil and balsamic vinegar (if using).
Sprinkle with a pinch of salt and pepper if desired.
4. **Serve:**
Serve immediately as a fresh and healthy snack for your toddler.

Nutritional Value per Serving (Approximate):

Calories: 80 Proteins: 4g Fats: 5g Carbohydrates: 3g

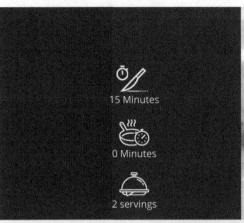

15 Minutes

0 Minutes

2 servings

Veggie Pinwheels

Ingredients:

·2 whole wheat or gluten-free tortillas
·1/4 cup hummus (store-bought or homemade)
·1/4 cup shredded carrots
·1/4 cup finely chopped bell peppers (any color)
·1/4 cup finely chopped cucumber
·1/4 cup baby spinach leaves
·1/4 cup shredded cheese (optional for non-vegan)

Practical Tips for Preparing and Planning Meals:

Batch Cooking: Prepare a larger batch and store leftovers in the refrigerator for quick snacks or meals.
Customization: Add other toddler-friendly vegetables like avocado, tomatoes, or finely chopped broccoli for variety.
Portable Snack: These pinwheels are great for on-the-go snacks or lunchboxes.

Storage Information:

Refrigerator: Store the prepared pinwheels in an airtight container for up to 2 days. The tortillas may become a bit soft, so it's best to serve them fresh.

Instructions:

1. **Prepare the Vegetables:**
Wash and finely chop the bell peppers and cucumber.
Shred the carrots.
2. **Spread the Hummus:**
Lay the tortillas flat on a clean surface.
Spread a thin, even layer of hummus over each tortilla, leaving about 1/2 inch around the edges.
3. **Add the Vegetables:**
Sprinkle the shredded carrots, chopped bell peppers, and cucumber evenly over the hummus on each tortilla.
Place the baby spinach leaves evenly on top of the vegetables.
If using, sprinkle shredded cheese over the vegetables.
4. **Roll and Slice:**
Starting at one end, tightly roll up each tortilla into a log shape.
Use a sharp knife to slice the rolled tortillas into 1-inch wide pinwheels.
5. **Serve:**
Arrange the pinwheels on a plate and serve immediately.

Nutritional Value per Serving (Approximate):
Calories: 120 Proteins: 4g Fats: 5g Carbohydrates: 15g

10 Minutes

10 Minutes

2 servings

English Muffin Pizzas

Ingredients:

·1 whole wheat English muffin (or gluten-free English muffin)
·1/4 cup marinara sauce or pizza sauce
·1/2 cup shredded mozzarella cheese (or dairy-free cheese)
·1/4 cup chopped vegetables (such as bell peppers, tomatoes, spinach, mushrooms)
·1/4 teaspoon dried oregano or Italian seasoning (optional)
·A pinch of salt and pepper (optional)

Practical Tips for Preparing and Planning Meals:

Batch Cooking: Prepare multiple English muffin pizzas and store leftovers in the refrigerator for quick snacks or meals.
Customization: Add other toddler-friendly toppings like pineapple, olives, or cooked chicken for variety.
Portable Snack: These mini pizzas are great for on-the-go snacks or lunchboxes.

Storage Information:

Refrigerator: Store the prepared mini pizzas in an airtight container for up to 2 days. Reheat gently in the oven or microwave before serving.

Instructions:

1.   **Preheat the Oven:**
Preheat your oven to 375°F (190°C). Grease a baking sheet gently or line it with parchment paper.
2.   **Prepare the English Muffins:**
Split the English muffin in half to create two round halves.
3.   **Assemble the Pizzas:**
Place the English muffin halves on the prepared baking sheet, cut side up.
Spread a thin layer of marinara sauce or pizza sauce on each muffin half.
Sprinkle the shredded mozzarella cheese evenly over the sauce.
Add the chopped vegetables on top of the cheese.
Sprinkle with dried oregano or Italian seasoning, and a pinch of salt and pepper if desired.
4.   **Bake the Pizzas:**
Bake in the preheated oven for about 10 minutes, or until the cheese is melted and bubbly, and the edges of the English muffins are golden brown.
5.   **Serve:**
Allow the mini pizzas to cool slightly before serving to your toddler.

Nutritional Value per Serving (Approximate):
Calories: 150 Proteins: 6g Fats: 5g Carbohydrates: 20g

10 Minutes

10 Minutes

4 servings

Stuffed Eggs

Ingredients:

·2 large eggs
·1 tablespoon plain Greek yogurt or dairy-free yogurt
·1 teaspoon mustard
·A pinch of salt (optional)
·A pinch of paprika (optional)
·1 teaspoon finely chopped chives or parsley (optional, for garnish)

Practical Tips for Preparing and Planning Meals:

Batch Preparation: Boil and peel the eggs ahead of time and store them in the refrigerator. Prepare the filling and assemble just before serving.
Customization: Add other mix-ins like finely chopped vegetables (e.g., bell peppers, cucumbers) or shredded cheese (dairy-free if needed) for extra nutrition and variety.
Portable Snack: These stuffed eggs are great for on-the-go snacks or lunchboxes.

Storage Information:

Refrigerator: Store the prepared stuffed eggs in an airtight container for up to 2 days. For best results, store the egg whites and filling separately and assemble just before serving.

Instructions:

1. **Boil the Eggs:**
Place the eggs in a small saucepan and cover them with cold water.
Bring the water to a boil over medium-high heat. Once the water is boiling, reduce the heat to low and simmer for 10 minutes. Remove the eggs from the saucepan and place them in a bowl of ice water to cool.
2. **Prepare the Eggs:**
Once the eggs are cool, peel them and slice them in half lengthwise.
Carefully remove the yolks and place them in a small bowl. Set the egg whites aside.
3. **Make the Filling:**
Mash the egg yolks with a fork until smooth. Add the plain Greek yogurt or dairy-free yogurt and mustard to the mashed yolks. Mix well to combine.
Season with a pinch of salt if desired.
4. **Stuff the Eggs:**
Spoon the yolk mixture back into the egg whites, dividing it evenly among the four halves.
Sprinkle with paprika and garnish with finely chopped chives or parsley if desired.
5. **Serve:**
Arrange the stuffed eggs on a plate and serve immediately as a fun and nutritious snack for your toddler.

Nutritional Value per Serving (Approximate):
Calories: 60 Proteins: 4g Fats: 4g Carbohydrates: 1g

DESSERTS

10 Minutes

0 Minutes

2 servings

Vegan Avocado Chocolate Pudding

Ingredients:

- 1 ripe avocado
- 2 tablespoons cocoa powder
- 2 tablespoons maple syrup or agave syrup
- 1/4 cup almond milk or any plant-based milk
- 1 teaspoon vanilla extract
- A pinch of salt
- Fresh berries or sliced banana for topping (optional)

Practical Tips for Preparing and Planning Meals:

Batch Cooking: Prepare a larger batch and store leftovers in the refrigerator for up to 2 days.
Customization: Add a tablespoon of nut butter for extra flavor and nutrition.
Texture Variety: For a smoother texture, ensure the avocado is very ripe and blend thoroughly.

Storage Information:

Refrigerator: Store the prepared pudding in an airtight container for up to 2 days. Stir well before serving.

Instructions:

1. **Prepare the Avocado:**
Cut the avocado in half, remove the pit, and scoop the flesh into a blender or food processor.
2. **Blend the Ingredients:**
Add the cocoa powder, maple syrup or agave syrup, almond milk, vanilla extract, and a pinch of salt to the blender or food processor.
Blend until smooth and creamy, scraping down the sides as needed to ensure everything is well combined.
3. **Adjust Consistency:**
If the pudding is too thick, add a little more almond milk, one tablespoon at a time, until you reach the desired consistency.
4. **Serve:**
Spoon the pudding into small bowls and top with fresh berries or sliced banana if desired.
Serve immediately or chill in the refrigerator for 15-20 minutes before serving.

Nutritional Value per Serving (Approximate):
Calories: 150 Proteins: 2g Fats: 10g Carbohydrates: 15g

10 Minutes

15 Minutes

12 servings

Banana Oat Cookies

Ingredients:

·2 ripe bananas, mashed
·1 cup rolled oats (gluten-free if needed)
·1/4 cup almond butter or peanut butter
·1/4 cup raisins or dairy-free chocolate chips
·1 teaspoon vanilla extract
·1/2 teaspoon ground cinnamon
·A pinch of salt (optional)

Practical Tips for Preparing and Planning Meals:

Batch Cooking: Prepare a larger batch and store leftovers in the refrigerator or freezer for quick snacks.
Customization: Add other mix-ins like chopped nuts, seeds, or dried fruit for variety.
Portable Snack: These cookies are great for on-the-go snacks or lunchboxes.

Storage Information:

Refrigerator: Store the prepared cookies in an airtight container for up to 3 days.
Freezer: Freeze the cooked cookies in a single layer on a baking sheet, then transfer to an airtight container and freeze for up to 1 month. Thaw in the refrigerator overnight before serving.

Instructions:

1. **Preheat the Oven:**
Preheat your oven to 350°F (175°C). Line a baking sheet with parchment paper.
2. *Prepare the Banana Mixture:*
In a large bowl, mash the ripe bananas until smooth.
3. **Combine Ingredients:**
Add the rolled oats, almond butter or peanut butter, raisins or dairy-free chocolate chips, vanilla extract, ground cinnamon, and a pinch of salt (if using) to the mashed bananas.
Mix until all ingredients are well combined.
4. *Form the Cookies:*
Scoop tablespoons of the mixture onto the prepared baking sheet, flattening each one slightly with the back of the spoon to form cookie shapes.
5. **Bake:**
Bake in the preheated oven for 12-15 minutes, or until the cookies are golden brown and firm to the touch.
6. **Serve:**
Allow the cookies to cool on the baking sheet for a few minutes before transferring them to a wire rack to cool completely.

Nutritional Value per Serving (Approximate):
Calories: 70 Proteins: 1g Fats: 2g Carbohydrates: 12g

15 Minutes

20-25 Minutes

12 servings

Gluten-Free Apple and Carrot Muffins

Ingredients:

- 1 cup gluten-free all-purpose flour
- 1/2 cup almond flour
- 1/2 teaspoon baking soda
- 1/2 teaspoon baking powder
- 1/2 teaspoon ground cinnamon
- 1/4 teaspoon ground nutmeg (optional)
- 1/4 teaspoon salt
- 2 large eggs
- 1/4 cup coconut oil, melted
- 1/4 cup honey or maple syrup
- 1 teaspoon vanilla extract
- 1 cup grated carrot (about 2 small carrots)
- 1 cup grated apple (about 1 medium apple)
- 1/4 cup unsweetened applesauce

Practical Tips for Preparing and Planning Meals:

Batch Cooking: Prepare a larger batch and store leftovers in the refrigerator or freezer for quick snacks.
Customization: Add finely chopped nuts or raisins for extra texture and flavor.
Texture Variety: For a smoother texture, finely grate the carrot and apple.

Storage Information:

Refrigerator: Store the prepared muffins in an airtight container for up to 3 days.
Freezer: Freeze the muffins in a single layer on a baking sheet, then transfer to an airtight container and freeze for up to 1 month. Thaw in the refrigerator overnight before serving.

Instructions:

1. **Preheat the Oven:**
Preheat your oven to 350°F (175°C). Line a muffin tin with paper liners or grease it lightly with coconut oil.
2. **Prepare the Dry Ingredients:**
In a large bowl, whisk together the gluten-free flour, almond flour, baking soda, baking powder, ground cinnamon, ground nutmeg (if using), and salt.
3. **Prepare the Wet Ingredients:**
In another bowl, whisk together the eggs, melted coconut oil, honey or maple syrup, vanilla extract, and applesauce.
4. **Combine Wet and Dry Ingredients:**
Pour the wet ingredients into the dry ingredients and stir until just combined. Fold in the grated carrot and grated apple.
5. **Fill the Muffin Tin:**
Spoon the batter evenly into the prepared muffin tin, filling each cup about 3/4 full.
6. **Bake the Muffins:**
Bake in the preheated oven for 20-25 minutes, or until a toothpick inserted into the center of a muffin comes out clean.
7. **Cool and Serve:**
Allow the muffins to cool in the tin for about 5 minutes, then transfer to a wire rack to cool completely before serving to your toddler.

Nutritional Value per Serving (Approximate):

Calories: 150 Proteins: 2g Fats: 6g Carbohydrates: 22g

10 Minutes

0 Minutes

10 servings

Frozen Yogurt Bark

Ingredients:

·2 cups plain Greek yogurt (or dairy-free yogurt)
·1-2 tablespoons honey or maple syrup (optional, for added sweetness)
·1/2 cup fresh berries (strawberries, blueberries, raspberries), chopped if large
·1/4 cup granola or crushed nuts (optional)
·1-2 tablespoons mini chocolate chips or dried fruit (optional)

Practical Tips for Preparing and Planning Meals:

Batch Preparation: Make a larger batch and store leftovers in the freezer for quick snacks.
Customization: Add other toddler-friendly toppings like shredded coconut, chia seeds, or a drizzle of nut butter for variety.
Portable Snack: These frozen yogurt bark pieces are great for on-the-go snacks or lunchboxes.

Storage Information:

Freezer: Store the prepared yogurt bark pieces in an airtight container or freezer bag for up to 1 month. Enjoy straight from the freezer.

Instructions:

1. **Prepare the Baking Sheet:**
Line a baking sheet with parchment paper.
2. **Mix the Yogurt:**
In a medium bowl, mix the Greek yogurt with honey or maple syrup if using. Stir until well combined.
3. **Spread the Yogurt:**
Pour the yogurt mixture onto the prepared baking sheet and spread it out evenly to about 1/4 inch thickness.
4. **Add the Toppings:**
Sprinkle the fresh berries evenly over the yogurt.
Add granola or crushed nuts, mini chocolate chips, or dried fruit if desired.
5. **Freeze:**
Place the baking sheet in the freezer for at least two hours, or until the yogurt is completely set and solid.
6. Break into Pieces:
Once frozen, remove the baking sheet from the freezer and break the yogurt bark into pieces.
7. **Serve:**
Serve immediately or store in a freezer-safe container.

Nutritional Value per Serving (Approximate):
Calories: 60 Proteins: 3g Fats: 2g Carbohydrates: 8g

10 Minutes

10 Minutes

16 servings

Rice Krispies Treats

Ingredients:

·3 tablespoons dairy-free butter or margarine
·1 package (10 ounces) marshmallows (use vegan marshmallows if needed)
·6 cups Rice Krispies cereal (gluten-free if needed)

Practical Tips for Preparing and Planning Meals:

Batch Preparation: Make a larger batch and store leftovers for quick snacks.
Customization: Add mix-ins like dairy-free chocolate chips, dried fruit, or sprinkles for variety.
Portable Snack: These treats are great for on-the-go snacks or lunchboxes.

Storage Information:

Refrigerator: Store the prepared Rice Krispies treats in an airtight container for up to 1 week.
Freezer: Freeze the treats in a single layer on a baking sheet, then transfer to an airtight container and freeze for up to 1 month. Thaw at room temperature before serving.

Instructions:

1. **Prepare the Pan:**
Grease a 9x13 inch baking pan with dairy-free butter or line it with parchment paper.
2. **Melt the Butter:**
In a large pot, melt the dairy-free butter over low heat.
3. **Add the Marshmallows:**
Add the marshmallows to the pot and stir until completely melted and smooth. This may take a few minutes.
4. **Mix in the Cereal:**
Remove the pot from the heat and gradually add the Rice Krispies cereal, stirring well to coat the cereal evenly with the melted marshmallow mixture.
5. **Transfer to Pan:**
Press the mixture evenly into the prepared baking pan. Use a greased spatula or wax paper to press it down firmly.
6. **Cool and Cut:**
Allow the Rice Krispies treats to cool completely in the pan. Once cooled, cut into small squares or rectangles.
7. **Serve:**
Serve the Rice Krispies treats immediately or store in an airtight container.

Nutritional Value per Serving (Approximate):
Calories: 90 Proteins: 1g Fats: 3g Carbohydrates: 16g

⏱🔪
10 Minutes

🍲⏲
0 Minutes

🛎
4 servings

Banana and Coconut Ice Cream

Ingredients:

·3 ripe bananas
·1/2 cup coconut milk (full-fat for creamier texture)
·1 tablespoon honey or maple syrup (optional, for added sweetness)
·1 teaspoon vanilla extract (optional)
·1/4 cup shredded coconut (optional, for topping)

Practical Tips for Preparing and Planning Meals:

Batch Preparation: Prepare a larger batch and store leftovers in the freezer for a quick and easy treat.
Customization: Add other mix-ins like chocolate chips, chopped nuts, or fruit pieces for variety.
Portable Snack: Scoop the ice cream into small containers for an easy, on-the-go treat.

Storage Information:

Freezer: Store the prepared ice cream in an airtight container in the freezer for up to 1 week. Allow it to sit at room temperature for a few minutes before scooping if it becomes too hard.

Instructions:

1. **Prepare the Bananas:**
Peel the bananas and slice them into small pieces.
2. **Freeze the Bananas:**
Place the banana slices on a baking sheet lined with parchment paper.
Freeze the banana slices for at least 2 hours or until completely frozen.
3. **Blend the Ingredients:**
In food processor or powerful blender, mix together the frozen banana pieces, coconut milk, honey or maple syrup (if you're using them), and vanilla extract (if you're using it). Blend until smooth and creamy, scraping down the sides as needed.
4. **Serve Immediately or Freeze:**
For soft-serve consistency, serve the banana and coconut ice cream immediately.
For a firmer texture, transfer the mixture to a freezer-safe container and freeze for an additional 1-2 hours. Stir the mixture every 30 minutes to maintain a creamy texture.
5. **Add Toppings:**
If desired, sprinkle shredded coconut on top of the ice cream before serving.

Nutritional Value per Serving (Approximate):
Calories: 100 Proteins: 1g Fats: 3g Carbohydrates: 18g

10 Minutes

5 Minutes

10 servings

Chocolate-Dipped Strawberries

Ingredients:

·8-10 fresh strawberries, washed and dried
·1/2 cup dark chocolate chips (dairy-free if needed)
·1 teaspoon coconut oil (optional, for smoother chocolate)

Practical Tips for Preparing and Planning Meals:

Batch Preparation: Prepare a larger batch and store leftovers in the refrigerator for a quick and easy snack.
Customization: Add a sprinkle of finely chopped nuts, shredded coconut, or sprinkles on the wet chocolate for added texture and flavor.
Portable Snack: These chocolate-dipped strawberries are great for special occasions and can be easily packed for picnics or parties.

Storage Information:

Refrigerator: Store the prepared chocolate-dipped strawberries in an airtight container in the refrigerator for up to 2 days.

Instructions:

1. **Prepare the Strawberries:**
After washing, pat strawberries dry with a paper towel. Make sure they are completely dry to ensure the chocolate sticks.
2. **Melt the Chocolate:**
In a microwave-safe bowl, combine the dark chocolate chips and coconut oil (if using). Microwave in 20-second intervals, stirring well after each interval, until the chocolate is completely melted and smooth.
3. **Dip the Strawberries:**
Hold each strawberry by the stem and dip it into the melted chocolate, turning it to coat evenly.
Allow any excess chocolate to drip off before placing the dipped strawberry on a baking sheet lined with parchment paper.
4. **Chill the Strawberries:**
Once all the strawberries are dipped, place the baking sheet in the refrigerator for about 15-20 minutes, or until the chocolate is set.
5. **Serve:**
Serve the chocolate-dipped strawberries immediately as a fun and nutritious treat for your toddler.

Nutritional Value per Serving (Approximate):
Calories: 50 Proteins: 0.5g Fats: 2g Carbohydrates: 8g

5 Minutes

0 Minutes

4 servings

Fruit Salad with Honey-Lime Dressing

Ingredients:

For the Fruit Salad:
- 1 cup strawberries, hulled and sliced
- 1 cup blueberries
- 1 cup pineapple, cut into small chunks
- 1 cup grapes, halved
- 1 kiwi, peeled and sliced
- 1 banana, sliced (add just before serving to prevent browning)

For the Honey-Lime Dressing:
- 2 tablespoons honey (use maple syrup for toddlers under 1 year old)
- 1 tablespoon fresh lime juice
- 1/2 teaspoon lime zest (optional)

Instructions:

1. **Prepare the Fruit:**
Wash and prepare all the fruit. Hull and slice the strawberries, halve the grapes, cut the pineapple into small chunks, peel and slice the kiwi, and slice the banana.

2. **Make the Dressing:**
In a small bowl, whisk together the honey (or maple syrup), fresh lime juice, and lime zest (if using).

3. **Combine the Ingredients:**
In a large bowl, combine all the prepared fruit except for the banana.
Drizzle the honey-lime dressing over the fruit and gently toss to combine.

4. **Serve:**
Just before serving, add the sliced banana to the fruit salad and give it a gentle toss.
Serve immediately as a refreshing and nutritious snack for your toddler.

Practical Tips for Preparing and Planning Meals:

Batch Preparation: Prepare the fruit and dressing ahead of time, but combine just before serving to maintain freshness.
Customization: Add other toddler-friendly fruits like mango, peach, or orange segments for variety.
Portable Snack: This fruit salad is great for on-the-go snacks or lunchboxes.

Storage Information:

Refrigerator: Store the prepared fruit salad in an airtight container for up to 1 day. Add the banana just before serving to prevent browning.

Nutritional Value per Serving (Approximate):
Calories: 100 Proteins: 1g Fats: 0g Carbohydrates: 25g

10 Minutes

5 Minutes

4 servings

Fruit Gelatin

Ingredients:

·2 cups 100% fruit juice (apple, grape, or orange juice work well)
·2 tablespoons agar-agar powder (for vegan) or 1 packet (0.25 ounces) unflavored gelatin
·1 cup mixed fresh fruit, chopped into small pieces (optional)

Practical Tips for Preparing and Planning Meals:

Batch Preparation: Make a larger batch and store leftovers in the refrigerator for quick snacks.
Customization: Use different fruit juices and add-ins like berries, grapes, or mandarin oranges for variety.
Portable Snack: These fruit gelatin pieces are great for on-the-go snacks or lunchboxes.

Storage Information:

Refrigerator: Store the prepared fruit gelatin in an airtight container in the refrigerator for up to 3 days.

Instructions:

1. **Prepare the Fruit Juice:**
Pour 1 cup of fruit juice into a medium saucepan. Sprinkle the agar-agar powder or gelatin over the juice and let it sit for a few minutes to bloom.
2. **Heat the Mixture:**
Place the saucepan over medium heat and stir the mixture until the agar-agar or gelatin is fully dissolved. This will take about 5 minutes. Do not let the mixture boil.
3. **Add Remaining Juice:**
Remove the saucepan from the heat and stir in the remaining 1 cup of fruit juice.
4. **Add Fresh Fruit (Optional):**
If using fresh fruit, distribute the fruit pieces evenly in your chosen molds or a shallow dish.
5. **Pour the Mixture:**
Pour the fruit juice mixture over the fruit in the molds or dish.
6. **Chill:**
Refrigerate for at least 2 hours, or until the gelatin is set.
7. **Serve:**
Once set, remove the gelatin from the molds or cut it into small squares if using a dish. Serve immediately.

Nutritional Value per Serving (Approximate):
Calories: 60 Proteins: 1g Fats: 0g Carbohydrates: 15g

10 Minutes

0 Minutes

4 servings

Mango Orange Sorbet

Ingredients:

·2 large ripe mangoes, peeled and chopped (about 2 cups of mango chunks)
·1 cup freshly squeezed orange juice (about 2-3 oranges)
·1 tablespoon honey or maple syrup (optional, for added sweetness)

Practical Tips for Preparing and Planning Meals:

Batch Preparation: Prepare a larger batch and store leftovers in the freezer for a refreshing treat anytime.
Customization: Add other fruits like pineapple, strawberries, or banana for variety.
Portable Snack: Scoop the sorbet into small containers for an easy, on-the-go treat.

Storage Information:

Freezer: Store the prepared sorbet in an airtight container in the freezer for up to 1 month. Allow it to sit at room temperature for a few minutes before scooping if it becomes too hard.

Instructions:

1. **Prepare the Ingredients:**
Peel and chop the mangoes into small pieces.
Squeeze the juice from the oranges.
2. **Blend the Ingredients:**
In a blender or food processor, combine the chopped mangoes, freshly squeezed orange juice, and honey or maple syrup (if using). Blend until smooth and creamy.
3. **Freeze the Mixture:**
Pour the mango-orange mixture into a shallow, freezer-safe dish.
Place the dish in the freezer for 3-4 hours, stirring the mixture every 30 minutes to break up any ice crystals and ensure a smooth texture.
4. **Serve:**
Once the sorbet is fully frozen, scoop it into small bowls and serve immediately.

Nutritional Value per Serving (Approximate):
Calories: 80 Proteins: 1g Fats: 0g Carbohydrates: 20g

Conclusion

As you close this chapter on "Pure & Simple: Healthy Kids Cuisine," we hope you're feeling empowered and excited about the journey of nourishing your child with wholesome, balanced meals. Mealtimes are more than just feeding moments; they're opportunities to create lasting memories, introduce new flavors, and instill lifelong healthy eating habits.

Throughout this book, we've provided you with a wide array of recipes that are not only nutritious but also easy to prepare and enjoy with your little ones. From breakfast to dinner, snacks to desserts, each dish is designed to be as delightful as it is nourishing, ensuring your child receives the essential nutrients they need to thrive.

Remember, the kitchen is a place of creativity, love, and connection. Involving your children in the cooking process, whether it's stirring, mixing, or simply choosing ingredients, can make mealtime a fun and educational experience. It's a chance to teach them about the importance of good nutrition, where their food comes from, and the joy of sharing a meal with loved ones.

Since each child is different and has different tastes and needs, we have included a variety of recipes in this book that may be modified to meet the nutritional demands of your family. Whether you're navigating food allergies, exploring new diets, or simply looking to introduce more variety into your child's meals, "Pure & Simple" is here to guide and support you.

As you continue to explore and experiment with these recipes, we encourage you to be patient and persistent, especially when introducing new foods to your child. It's okay if they don't love everything right away—taste buds evolve, and with your gentle encouragement, they'll gradually expand their palate.

Thank you for allowing us to be a part of your family's culinary journey. We hope that "Pure & Simple: Healthy Kids Cuisine" becomes a cherished resource in your kitchen, one that you return to time and time again for inspiration, guidance, and joy.

Here's to many more happy, healthy, and delicious moments around your family table. Bon appétit!

Made in the USA
Las Vegas, NV
06 October 2024

96359649R00069